Passenger train No. 7, the *Panoramic Limited*, double-heading with two T-29 class 4-6-0's, met No. 8, the eastbound section of the *Panoramic Limited* with engine No. 778, in a head-on collision at 2:58 P.M., August 20, 1925, near milepost 255 on the Royal Gorge Line. — R. P. PARSONS COLLECTION

CALL THE BIG HOOK

Samuel A. Dougherty

Golden West Books
San Marino, California

CALL THE BIG HOOK

Copyright © 1984 by Samuel A. Dougherty
All Rights Reserved
Published by Golden West Books
San Marino, California 91108 U.S.A.
Library of Congress Catalog Card No. 84-21224
I.S.B.N. 0-87095-087-8

Library of Congress Cataloging in Publication Data

Dougherty, Samuel A., 1917-
  Call the Big Hook.
  Includes Index.
    1. Railroads—United States—Accidents.
    2. Railroads—United States   Safety Measures.
    3. Denver and Rio Grande Western Railroad.
      I. Title
HE1780.D58 1984   363.1'22'0973   84-21224
ISBN   0-87095-087-8

READER'S NOTE

The text of this volume is loaded with railroaders' lingo, or the language of the working railroad man. Such jargon, like that of the lumberjack, the truck driver, or medical practitioner, is reflected in his speech. If these words seem confusing, a glossary of railroad words and terms may be found between pages 242-252.

ACKNOWLEDGMENTS

For picture material contributed to this book, either their own photographic artistry or from collections of which they are the owners or custodians, the author is indebted to the following: Gerald M. Best, John Crawford, Donald Duke, Ronald C. Hill, Henry R. Griffiths, Jr., Richard H. Kindig, John Krause, Sandra House Neiderhauser, John B. Norwood, R. P. Parsons, Al Rose, Robert W. Richardson, Fred Schneider, S. D. Smith, and Jackson Thode.

To Joe Harris of the D&RGW, I thank him for the profiles and the prints. Also to John Signor for the beautiful cover design and the maps which depict two of the accidents mentioned in this book.

Golden West Books

A Division of Pacific Railroad Publications, Inc.

P.O. BOX 80250 • SAN MARINO, CALIFORNIA • 91108-8250

To

MariAnn and John who asked me to write it all down,
And
For Wendell and Bud who said I should.

"Sampson de Grande," crane No. 028, in action at Green River, Utah. Trainmaster John B. Norwood, in the suit, hat and white shirt, is supervising the reopening of the mainline and the clean up operation.
—JOHN B. NORWOOD COLLECTION

PREFACE

"Call the Big Hook" is the order given by the Denver & Rio Grande Western Railroad chief dispatcher to the mechanical department when a disaster strikes the railroad. In the old days this notice was hammered out by Morse Code over the telegraph, but today the message is issued verbally by telephone or over the radio. Those four words set in motion a flurry of activity like a military attack. "Call the Big Hook" involves crew dispatchers and enginehouse foremen, car foremen and roadmasters, engineers and firemen, and train crews consisting of conductors and brakemen. Every employee called for wrecker service drops everything and rushes to man the giant derrick used to clear the track. Pure and simple it is a mobilization of railroad forces, and every second counts in a disaster, whether it is a slide, rear-ender, or a wash out.

The only significant safety innovations on the railroad since the invention of the Westinghouse air brake, the automatic block system and electric interlocking, has been the train radio and Centralized Traffic Control (CTC). In actual practice CTC is more a method of increasing track capacity than a safety device. It can hardly be expected that all these devices will eliminate accidents, for their very effect at making train movements faster, multiplies the potential danger they create.

"Call The Big Hook" is a true story. The disasters presented on the following pages are known fact. In a few cases the author had to speculate and assume what really did happen from his years of experience working for the Denver & Rio Grande Western Railroad. The railroad industry is very safety conscious. In spite of the fact of strict compliance with the *Operating Book of Rules*, accidents do happen that are either acts of God or man-made. It is my purpose to show how the railroad works and operates in a crisis. It is not the intent of the author to indict any employee nor accuse the company of negligence.

The fabric of the author's family life has been influenced by this fascinating railroad industry through four generations. Railroaders are a breed apart. When railroad men are involved in the movement of trains, in keeping schedules, or aid to another railroad man at the scene of an accident, there is loyalty and dedication. My father used to say, "Anything can happen on a railroad and it usually does." No doubt an early version of Murphy's Law.

I may quote a few passages from the Book of Rules, and furnish data, but the reader must make up his or her own mind as to the cause and effect of the accidents presented. When anything goes wrong in life, or even with your car for that matter, it is appropriate to say a few strong words to relieve the frustration. It does work! Herein, I have used some profanity for descriptive purposes only. As a railroad man who learns of the derailment of an 80-car freight train, with 35 cars in the ditch and 500 feet of track torn up — what can one say?

This book is primarily historical, since all of the events have taken place. Its major purpose is to entertain. I hope that "Call the Big Hook" will illustrate the evolution of railroad safety practices the Denver & Rio Grande Western Railroad has made during my lifetime.

S.A. Dougherty

Lakewood, Colorado
September 1984

Table of Contents

Looking north at Helper, Utah. Castle Gate and the eastern ascent of Solider Summit is located in the division of the Wasatch range at the left. The 14-stall roundhouse is located at the bend in the track. The two story station may be seen at the left of the coaling tower. — GEORGE ANDERSON—JACKSON

THODE COLLECTION

1

"Helper, Utah."

TEANCUM PRATT, a Mormon pioneer, was an enterprising man of great foresight. While prospecting for coal in the Price River Canyon in 1870, he located his two wives in a rude dugout in a grove of cottonwood trees that grew along the stream at the west end of Castle Valley in eastern Utah. Pratt found a rich deposit of coal and platted a mining town that was to bear his name, Pratt City. Acquiring much of the surrounding real estate, he would later sell land for a right-of-way and terminal facility to the Denver & Rio Grande Railroad.

The new rail line was built narrow-gauge to Salt Lake City in March of 1883. A coaling facility, water tank, enginehouse and hotel were built in Pratt City. The line was converted to standard gauge in 1890, and because it was necessary to use additional motive power to help the heavy trains to the top of the Wasatch on a 2.4 percent grade, the pushers, or helpers were stationed at the foot of the hill, and the name of the little town was changed to Helper.

So Helper was correctly, if oddly renamed. The small community was one street wide and was located between the river and the railroad in a narrow canyon running through the low, cedar and pinon covered foothills. North of the town rises a vertical wall of red sandstone, towering over a thousand feet, forming a barrier of imposing beauty. On the top of the escarpment, at its western end, sets a huge boulder as large as an office building. It is perched in a precarious balance, and is aptly named "The Balanced Rock." God alone knows how long it has stood in that position. The pious local citizens have been expecting the rock to fall and destroy their community for its wicked ways ever since Helper became a town.

For a small community it did have wicked ways. At one time the place boasted 21 saloons on its mile long main street. Whores and gamblers catered to the passions the bartenders couldn't handle. Saturday nights, holidays, and just plain paydays were occasions for raising hell in that place, sometimes with fatal results. Fist fights between the coal miners and railroad men were common. Gun fights and stabbings happened once in a while, too. The town marshall had several notches on his .38 pistol as a result of settling disputes and solving crimes.

Beneath those sandstone rims and cedar flats lay some of the largest coal deposits in the west. Mines were opened in the late 1800's and the early 1900's. This gave the railroad its principal source of tonnage and furnished the only other major industry in Carbon County. That is, in addition to the whores and gamblers. There was a bakery and the usual shops and stores found in a small town. My grandmother ran a cafe there for many years. Helper was a mine and railroad oriented community.

Grandmother McComb told us kids of the time when "Butch" Cassidy and his infamous gang from the Hole-in-the-Wall ate in her place prior to their visit to the office of the Utah Fuel Company in Castle Gate. That little unsocial call cost the mine company $8,500.00 in gold!

Grandfather McComb was an Irish immigrant who came over on a ship only one step ahead of enforced service in Her Royal Majesty's Army. He moved west as a laborer on the railroad, and advanced to the position of section foreman, or "King Snipe." He had a gang of Chinese laborers working for him at Woodside, Utah, where in 1890 my mother, Mary, was born in a company owned section house beside the main track. At the time, my grandmother was cooking for the section crew.

It was during the year of my mother's birth that the railroad converted its narrow-gauge track to standard gauge. We have been told that the entire conversion was accomplished in only one day! Quite a feat, considering it was all done by hand labor. Standard gauge ties, which were much longer, had already been placed in the track. The rails were unspiked and spread to the standard width and then respiked. The changeover merely required moving rails and switches at each siding.

Our family home in Helper was located just across the county road from the main line of the Denver & Rio Grande Railroad, and somewhat southwest of the "roundhouse," or Mallet house where the steam locomotives were serviced. This is where the steam derrick, or wrecker, as we called it, was kept on standby for emergencies.

Our house was an ugly, little frame structure, originally built to house a lumber yard. It sat right on the main street; there was no frontage or yard. The front door opened on the sidewalk. It was so close to the roadway you could hear the clop-clop of the horses hoofs as they passed, pulling wagons on the thoroughfare. A typically western building with a sloping roof and a false front, it was constructed of shiplap lumber that had never known paint. Electricity had been wired in as an afterthought. The twisted wire drop cords hung from the center of the ceiling of each room. There were no wall plugs or wall switches in those days. The clear glass bulbs that we used had little teats on them, and they really did look like a hairpin burning in a bottle. As I remember, they did not provide much illumination. We kept kerosene lamps and wax candles on hand for emergencies as the local power source was prone to frequent and prolonged failures. Hooked rag rugs covered the bare floors in four of the five rooms in the house which kept the slivers from sticking in our bare feet. The kitchen floor was covered with a slick, shiny sheet of material called "con-go-le-um." It was easy to keep clean, but cold to walk on. Heating was provided by the cooking stove in the kitchen and by a "Round Oak" heater in the living room. All of the stoves burned coal, a pile of which was dumped on the ground off to the right side of the back door.

The location of the family home was real handy for my dad, who was an engineer for the Rio Grande. He could take his calls

The impact of railroad station architecture on the American imagination is reflected in this scene of the Helper depot. The structure housed the agent/operator, the telegraph office, the waiting room, and the baggage room. — S. A. DOUGHERTY COLLECTION

Overall scene of the station grounds at Helper. The Railroad YMCA is the two story stone structure at the left. The D&RGW depot is the peaked roof structure on the right. — S. A. DOUGHERTY COLLECTION

for service, put his work clothes on, eat, and get to the roundhouse before the crew caller had time to call the other crewmen and return to his office.

Dad did not like to be late for work. He would always report early for duty, taking lots of time and great care to oil and inspect his engine. As a result of this habit he had a good reputation for having few delays or engine failures. At retirement he had 37 years of service without an accident or serious derailment.

As far as my mother was concerned, the house we lived in was located in a very poor place. When the wind was right it carried with it a great amount of dust, coal smoke and cinders picked up from the rail yards. Keeping house was a full-time job for her. Fighting grime and cooking short-order meals for a working hoghead was an almost never-ending chore. Clean, crisp curtains at the windows remained so for only two or three days. Wall paper patterns faded under layers of smoke in a matter of weeks, but mother did not complain much. She just kept on trying to keep the family and that ugly little house clean. Washing clothes must have been difficult, using a scrub-board and obtaining hot water which had to be heated in a copper boiler on a coal fired cook stove.

My father's overalls were always starched and ironed. Mother said it helped to keep them clean longer and starch sure made them shine. In addition to her tasks of cleaning and cooking, she took care of six kids. We were of some help with such things as carrying in coal and kindling, and taking out water and ashes. There was water piped into the house, but it had no sewer or toilet facilities, thus disposal presented several problems. The big tin wash tubs served as bath tubs on Saturday nights, and a "Chick Sale" with its two-holer seat became a comedy routine after the advent of indoor plumbing. In that day and time it was no laughing matter.

The piercing blasts of the steam whistle echoed loudly in the narrow canyon. Three long, three short, repeated three times was the signal that was sounded from the railroad powerhouse whistle to alert the "car toads" of an emergency on the line which required calling the Big Hook. It was an eerie and frightening sound when you were a child lying in your bed at night and your father was out on a run. Someone has had a wreck!

Compound No. 1069 waits at Helper for the next freight to ascend Soldier Summit. This Class L-96 2-8-8-2 was built by Schenectady in 1913. — s. a. DOUGHERTY COLLECTION

Locomotive No. 1213 has just come in from a run and rests at the Helper roundhouse. Baldwin built this K-59 class 2-8-2 in 1919. This particular locomotive, scrapped in 1955, provided the D&RGW with 43 years of faithful service. — s. a. DOUGHERTY COLLECTION

A turn of the century Rio Grande Western "Big Hook" stationed at Helper had hemp rope for cables and the car arch bar trucks. The unknown gentleman wears typical railroad attire of the time and his lady is decked out in her Sunday best complete with plummed hat. — S. A. DOUGHERTY COLLECTION

Four giant 2-8-8-2's are lined up outside the Helper roundhouse for service on Soldier Summit. Nos. 1074-1066-1069 had 57-inch drivers and 26 & 40x32-inch cylinders. These engines became Nos. 3414-3406-3409 respectively in a 1924 renumbering. — S. A. DOUGHERTY COLLECTION

The second batch of big Mallet compounds arrived from Schenectady in 1913 for use on Soldier Summit. Nos. 1068 and 1072 shown in this scene at Helper were later renumbered to Nos. 3408 and 3412. — s. a. dougherty collection

One of the principal concerns of any railroad family was that father might get killed or injured in a collision or a derailment. Accidents were commonplace, and my early memories of hearing the roundhouse foreman blow that steam whistle are vivid.

It was a popular practice in those days for a local photographer to visit the scene of a wreck and record on film the destruction of track and equipment. He would then hawk copies of his pictures printed on postcard size paper, and suitable for mailing. My family collected a number of these, and as a child I spent hours looking at them; fascinated and yet horrified by the scenes of devastation. Piles of twisted iron and splintered wood; of overturned locomotives and washed out track and bridges. It was no wonder that I was frightened when I heard that roundhouse whistle blow.

I must have been about eight years old when I saw my first big train wreck up close. It was a dandy, too! No one was hurt, but it was a hair-raising pileup, nonetheless. The cars involved were refrigerator cars loaded with ripe fruit such as oranges, peaches, grapes and pears. The exciting part was all of us kids got to see the wreck and to help salvage the spilled produce.

Every fall the railroad handled long trains of bright yellow, iced "reefers" of fruit from the California valleys to markets in the east. I can still remember those colorful trains snaking their way downgrade off Soldier Summit, and the trailing clouds of blue smoke from the pressure of brake shoes against the wheels. All trains had to have their car retaining valves set in a heavy holding position when descending the mountain grade. The trains all stopped right in front of our house so the trainmen could knock down the "pops." A crew change was made at Helper while the car toads inspected each car journal box for waste pack and oil level. Each wheel was also checked for defects, such as cracks, broken flanges, or excessive heating.

On one particular day in August 1926, this big eastbound fruit block, trailing blue smoke and the perfume of ripening fruit, stopped for inspection in Helper. Someone obviously missed a broken flange on a wheel, because about a mile east of the yard the train derailed. Broken and battered cars were strewn along the right-of-way.

A bunch of us kids were swimming in the Price River at the time, and when we heard the noise and saw the commotion, we quickly pulled on our clothes. There were no swim suits to worry about or slow us down in those days. We ran to see what had happened!

Boy, what a mess! The yellow reefers were torn open and boxes of ripe fruit were spilled everywhere amid the wreckage. Naturally we helped ourselves to this windfall supply of fresh fruit until the "cinder dicks" chased us away. Some of the town's merchants bought the salvage from the railroad and hired us urchins to help transfer the undamaged boxes from the wrecked rail cars to highway trucks. A lot of those grapes were later stomped into homemade wine. We all got paid for our help . . . in ripe fruit!

I had picked ripe fruit for a nickel a box, shoveled snow, cut wood, and relieved the regular newspaper delivery boy on his vacation, but I never worked on a regular or salaried basis until I went to work for the railroad as a Mechanical Department laborer at Helper, Utah, in August 1937. The job paid .39 cents an hour and you broke in on your own time. Most of my railroad work in those early years was performed at night and on a call basis. It was not a very good job, but it was a good place to start. While the conditions were poor, it had a future so I was told. If I worked diligently and kept my nose clean, I could someday hope to be promoted to locomotive fireman, and eventually to engineer, like my dad.

All my life I had watched my father work nights and holidays, going out on the railroad in all extremes of weather. He would come home greasy from breakdowns, muddy from washouts, and even bloody, like the time his engine struck an automobile. He became bloodstained while removing the victims from the wreckage that piled up on the front of his locomotive. And I had vowed, "No way. No, never. No, not for me. No!" But four years of depression convinced me that any job was a good job, even if it meant getting a "tin bill" and picking with the chickens, just so long as it paid, and there were prospects for something better down the road.

I never quite understood the advice "to keep my nose clean" on the job. Everything about railroad work at that level was dirty, dusty, greasy, big, hot, heavy, sharp, dull, obstinate, or any combination of the afore listed. Keeping clean was impossible. Steam engines made smoke and created ashes. They needed oil and grease. Coal dust was a by-product of standing in the deck, swinging a Number Four scoop. Obviously, "to keep my nose clean" meant to keep out of trouble.

Performing many of the duties of a laborer helped to qualify an employee as a locomotive fireman later on. One learned how to operate a stoker, work feedwater pumps and injectors, drain and fill hydrostatic lubricators — where the flange oilers were located, how they were filled and what supplies were necessary to carry on the engine — like a coalpick, scoop shovel, clinkerhook, shaker bar, ashpan hoe, jet cleaning rod, alligator wrench, tool box, fusees, torpedoes, red and white lanterns, grease gun and pin dope, a red flag, two white and two green flags as well. When you were the supplyman it was your duty to check all of this stuff and provide anything that was needed. You were also the engine watchman, and that required you to shovel in enough coal to keep the fire and the steam pressure up, and the water in the boiler at a safe level.

When business was good and they were running a lot of trains, the supplyman might service 16 or 18 engines in an eight-hour shift while also performing the watchman's duties at the same time. There was no opportunity to get bored.

Working nights was scary for the beginner. The inside of the enginehouse was as dark as a weasel's bedroom and always filled with smoke and steam. Men walking in the clouds of foggy mist seemed oversized and ethereal. Those old Mallet air pumps would wheeze, thump and pound, making all sorts of weird noises.

There were eight stalls across the house and each segment had a four foot deep, concrete-lined inspection pit. One had to be very cautious not to step in one of them in the dark. It was a rude shock to feel yourself falling, with nothing under your feet, and then having your chest crunch against the lip of a gaping hole.

To fill the locomotive lubricators, it was necessary to carry ten gallons of oil in two long spout cans from the storehouse. You signed for the supplies, then carried it over to the engine that needed valve and engine oil. Next you got a ten-foot high ladder to reach the level of the reservoir, lugging the cans with you. The reservoir trap was opened and you poured in the lubricant. And don't spill it!

Roundhouse laborers were required to clean fires in the locomotives after the road crews or hostlers had placed the engines on the firepit. Servicing the stationary boiler that supplied power for the machine shop was also one of the duties. Both of these jobs were hot and dirty work, but preferable to working at the sandhouse and the coal chute. They were the "pits."

The company got "boney coal" free from the mines for hauling it away. This refuse came in big lumps that were too large to pass through the coal gates on a steam engine. When we dumped it on the grizzlies in the coal chute hopper it was necessary to break the big chunks into smaller pieces, by using a ten pound sledge. Eight hours of swinging that hammer was guaranteed to give you an appetite and make blisters on your hands.

A locomotive used sand for traction. Each engine had sand

Railroad wrecks, especially before the introduction of modern safety devices such as the air brake, were frequently horrible and dramatic, and the insistances of gross negligence which have sometimes been uncovered by subsequent investigations have hardly been such to inspire confidence in the railroad as a means of transport. But those early black marks in the record book should not obscure recognition that the record as a whole in this century has been a creditable one, and that the safety achievement of the American railroads has been greatly improved over the years. An accident, when it occurs, can be traced to some definitely ascertainable cause, whereas highway accidents can be explained only by the ambiguous words "lost control of vehicle."

One of the most spectacular wrecks on any railroad is the runaway. Many are caused by brake failure, the engineer's lack of judgement and his eventual loss of control of his train, or the failure to set retainers. It is near impossible to control the momentum on a mountain railroad, such as the Denver & Rio Grande Western, once it gets started.

The wreck in these three scenes took place on Soldier Summit in 1916. As a boy your author was fascinated with these post card pictures, yet horrified by the scenes of devastation and the tales told by railroad men of the accident. Today the details of this wreck are lost history as they are not recorded in the trade journals. This accident piled cars deep in the cut at Scenic Siding. The story is told one brakeman was killed in the accident.

— ALL S. A. DOUGHERTY COLLECTION

Engineer Leo Pender with Rio Grande Western No. 1184 at Helper, Utah, in 1906. Locomotives Nos. 1180-1199 were originally built for the RGW and, in 1908 were incorporated into the D&RG roster without a change in engine number. — S. A. DOUGHERTY COLLECTION

boxes on top of its boiler for storage. Dry sand was fed to the rails ahead of each drive wheel through one-inch pipes. In order for the material to flow freely and insure proper feed, it had to be dry. That is where I came into the picture. My first day's work for the railroad was in the sandhouse.

Outside the sandhouse was a long, deep pit where the supply of sand was unloaded by hand from open top gondolas for storage. The sand was invariably wet, or soon got that way from being out in the weather. It had to be dried.

STEP ONE: Unload wet sand from rail car into storage pile.

STEP TWO: Load wet sand into a wheelbarrow with a scoop shovel and then wheel it up an inclined plank walkway for 50 feet to the sandhouse and dump it on the concrete floor near the drying stoves.

STEP THREE: Wheel in a big load of lump coal and build a roaring fire in the stoves. There were two of them; capacity was one-ton of sand each. The stoves were enclosed by a funnel-shaped iron jacket. The top of the container was seven feet above the floor, the bottom was three feet high.

STEP FOUR: Using a Wyoming Red Edge, Number Four scoop, throw the wet sand from the floor into the big hopper that

24

surrounds the fire box. Fill it full, heaping it around the red-hot stack.

STEP FIVE: As the sand lost its moisture it ran freely from the small vents in the bottom of the jacket. This was a gift of gravity and the only break you got.

STEP SIX: Now scoop the dried sand off the floor and up over a coarse screen to remove the large particles before the sand runs into a big metal drum. When the drum was filled a manually operated valve was closed and another valve supplying compressed air was opened to blow the dry sand through a pipe that led to a storage bin located in the top of the coal chute.

Every grain of sand was handled five times. It used to make me furious to see an engineer open the sand valve on his engine, and then forget to close it. I knew full well what it took in sweat and strain to put the stuff in that box.

Within a year, the pay was increased to .43 cents per hour and Railroad Retirement became a reality. We were making great progress. In my spare time I made many student trips as a fireman, at my own expense and without compensation. I wanted to learn the road and how to make steam, not alibis.

I was in love with my job. I liked the work, the company and the men I was working with. It was hard, dirty work, but I stuck it out, and it paid off for me.

One cold, wintery night I was busily engaged in cleaning cinders and ash from the main track where we cleaned the fires and dumped the ashpans on the run-through passenger engines, using a scoop shovel and a wheelbarrow in my labors. It was snowing hard when one of the "old head" firemen I knew came by and offered me some encouragement.

He said, "Stick with it, kid, you will have a better job soon."

And I did get a better job. Perseverance paid off.

I retired from my labors after 42 years of service with no dismissals, no demerits and no reprimands, as I progressed from mechanical department laborer to locomotive fireman, to engineer, to Road Foreman of Equipment, to Trainmaster, to Division Assistant Superintendent and to Superintendent of Safety-Rules-Training of the Colorado Division.

If I have proved anything, it is this: Hard work will not kill you.

In 1911 the Rio Grande management had this celebrated and spectacular photograph of its crack *Panoramic Limited* taken on the ruling grade at Soldier Summit, Utah, where one road engine and four helpers were required to get eleven steel coaches and Pullmans over the hump. The scene was posed for Salt Lake photographer Harry Shipler, who was the official photographer of the RGW at the time. — GERALD M. BEST COLLECTION

2

Boomer Engineer

MY *FATHER* was an Irishman, and I am sure that if he had stayed in Donegal, he would have been a "shancie." They were the storytellers, the keepers of facts and fiction as it was told from generation to generation, preserving their history in the spoken word. The early Irish never had a written language.

Dad had a wonderful memory for names, places and events, especially names. After railroading for 50 years on lines all across the country, he could still recall the names of the sidings on the old CO&G where he had first worked. The Choctaw, Oklahoma & Gulf was later made part of the Iron Mountain division of the Missouri Pacific System.

His experience included service on 26 rail lines in the United States, Mexico and Canada as a "boomer" engineer. Incidentally, he was born and raised in the backwoods of Arkansas in the period following the Civil War. How I wish I had a tape recorder in those days, or even the foresight to write down the stories he told while we were sitting around the supper table. At the time there was no other form of entertainment, such as radio or television, and money was scarce for movies, so dad kept us amused with his

C. W. Dougherty, at the right with the oil can in hand, is the author's father. In 1895 he was the engineer on No. 396 of the Choctaw, Oklahoma & Gulf at Argenta, Arkansas. This 4-4-0 type locomotive was built by Rogers in 1868 for the Union Pacific Eastern District as No. 28 the *New Mexico*. It later became Kansas Pacific No. 28, and later on Union Pacific No. 396 in 1885. When it was obtained by the COG is not known. —S. A. DOUGHERTY COLLECTION

stories. Many of the tales were strictly "tall," but there was truth in some. I learned many years later, while on a trip down south, he had exaggerated somewhat, when I had a chance to meet the characters who populated his scenarios.

My dad had a nickname for nearly everyone who worked for the railroad. These sobriquets were hung on the man on account of his initials, his stature, some physical attribute, or because of an event. There were three engineers named Jones, so to keep the record straight and to distinguish these gentlemen, P.C. Jones was called "Pisscutter," C.S. Jones was called "Chicken Shit," and C.T. Jones was "Chew Tobacco" Jones. There was "Raw Meat," R.M. Newman and "Pistol Joe" Newman. He really carried a pistol and the story is told that once he shot Grover Coleman in the leg with it, although I always thought it was an accident. "Pistol Joe" had a great horn of a nose; maybe it just looked big on him because he stood about five-foot six inches and would weigh around 110 pounds. That is, if he was soaking wet and carried a car knuckle. There was "Old Cradle Face" Al Deason and "Jug Head" Smith, and "Kidney Foot," and "Goose Neck" and "Humpy" as well as one "Big Arky" Mitchell, whose first job, as dad told it, was "poling hogs" down in Arkansas. Mitch was big enough and strong enough to tie a thin razorback hog to the end of a long pole and then hold it up high enough in an oak tree so the hog could feed on the acorns. "Big Rodger" Reynolds was six-foot six and had an Irish brogue so thick he could hardly talk at all. "Little Joe" Rawlings was of average size and "Big Bill" Goddard measured five-foot one, but a hell of an engineman and a giant of spirit and intellect. There were "Shanty" O'Brien and "Stutterin' Bill" of the same name. "Slabs" Montoro and "Red" Snyder; "Bull Moose" Lindsley was a dead ringer for Teddy Roosevelt. I remember how the "Moose" always carried a shiny, new hayburner (a kerosene lantern) in place of a flashlight. "Scotty" Groesbeck and "Cocky" McCall, for obvious reasons.

My father told me of one guy named John Luther Jones who had worked for the old Illinois Central at the same time he had worked there. He had a service letter to substantiate that tall tale. He told how Jones got the nickname of "Casey" and became immortalized in song and legend.

"Suit Case Bill" Roberts moved around the division a lot as he

This scene is the result of the Schofield Dam disaster in Utah during June of 1917. The D&RGW was washed out in Price River Canyon at several locations. — S. A. DOUGHERTY COLLECTION

did not have much seniority. "Fat" McDaniels was obese and so was old man "Fat" Perry. "Pokey" Cowan could make a schedule though, and "Swift-foot" Needham couldn't. There was one he called "The Devil," who I thought was a nice old man when I met him in Little Rock many years ago. Age had probably mellowed him a great deal. There was "Skeeter" Weyer and "Toots" Ault and "Dutch" Weikel. "My man, Jim" Charlesworth was a Cockney Englishman, and his wife's description of him stuck as a nickname. There was "Smokey" House and "Smokey" Taylor and "Smokey" White, all so called for very good reasons, I assume. Good firemen tried to fire their engines with a clear stack. "Cautious Harry" Chambers surely earned his handle as a most careful runner.

The hoghead called "Dirty Neck" had one of the most uncomplimentary titles. One man was called "Bear Tracks" because of his No. 14 sized shoes. When he sat down and put his feet up it looked like two little boys were sitting in front of him. "Old Dog-leg" Parson Addams kept his knees bent when he walked. He did sort of look like a dog walking upright.

The official family was not neglected. Note one "Big Dan" Cunningham, the Master Mechanic. "Blondy" Wilcox, the Superintendent and E.H. "Silver Tip" Blackwell. "Liver Lip" Al Baxter was the Traveling Hoghead. They were a colorful lot and the old man could tell exciting and interesting stories about them all.

There were songs, too. Like *The Wreck of the Old 97, The Ballad of "Casey" Jones, The Engineer's Dream* and the poem *The Dying Hogger's Last Request*. I will fill you in on these a little farther on down the line.

An old railroad song called *The Engineer's Dream* seemed like it had been written about the Eden wreck that happened just north of Pueblo, Colorado, the night of August 7, 1904. As the story goes an early day passenger train, running through a blinding rain storm, ran into a washed out bridge and 88 passengers died. The locomotive and its crew were lost along with several coaches swept away in the flood. The words of the song go something like this.

An old grey haired man sat adreaming,
Alone by his fireside so bright.
While outside the door it was storming
And the wind howled a song thru the night.

He dreamed of his son on his engine,
The fastest express on the line.
He dreamed that he sat there beside him
As they sped thru the night making time.

And then when they came to the river,
He knew this would be their last run
For there in the darkness of midnight
He saw that the bridge had washed down.

He awoke from his dreaming,
Alone by his fireside agleam
And he did not give heed to the warning
For he thought it was only a dream.

And then thru the night came a message
That told him his dream had been true.
His brave son had gone to his Maker,
Along with the rest of the crew.

Oh, give heed to each warning,
For we know not how soon it will be
That the last call will come from the Master
And we go to that home o're the sea.

— Anon

There have been many times in the past when those lines came to my mind as my own locomotive roared over the line in periods of rain and flash floods. The East Utah desert is well-known for cloudbursts and the track and bridges have washed out on many occasions. I've been behind several wash outs, but luckily I was never involved in one. I did have a few near misses, though, like the time the No. 1601 on First 38 went through the bridge just west of Cisco, Utah, on October 13, 1941.

It had been raining for a whole week, it seemed. Normally the desert is a dry place; weeks and months go by without a drop. I came east on a fruit block, firing a Mallet for McConnell about twelve hours ahead of Murphy's crew on the ill-fated No. 1601. The sky was leaking badly across the subdivision; a steady, hard, soaking rain. A regular "toad-strangling" downpour. The clouds hung low and grey-black. The adobe dunes glistened in the eerie light.

Around three in the morning, the night operator at Cisco displayed a red order board for First No. 38. When the big, Mountain-type engine's headlight came around the right-hand curve west of the west switch, the operator saw the beam stab through the gloom for a short time. As the train reached the Cisco Wash, he saw the light shoot skyward and heard the rending crash as the mighty M-75 type collapsed the span. The engine broke away from its tender and plunged forward on her right side, crushing engineer W.E. Murphy to death beneath the right side cab window. Fireman A.A. Goodell was trapped in the splintered cab by the trailing cars of lumber. The tender, trucks and all, disappeared in the hole where the bridge had been. I was out there at the scene of the wreck on the Big Hook for a week after the accident and we never did find that tank . . . It is still in the hole created by the flood. Goodell lost all of his teeth and was battered and bruised, but he survived. The head end brakeman, A.A. Stuart, who was riding in the "doghouse" on the back of the tank of the No. 1601 made it. This trainman had just stepped out of his shanty on top of the cistern to get a look at the order board as the bridge collapsed under the engine and he found himself being swept away in the roiling waters. He was able to claw his way ashore at a highway bridge a quarter of a mile down stream; alive and full of muddy water.

There were 39 cars piled up in that mess; lumber, airplane parts, apples, sugar, and canned goods. Some of the box cars were washed down stream 300 yards, just to give you an idea of the force of a desert cloudburst and flash flooding. This was the first time I had ever seen bulldozers used around a wreck. There was no other way to coax those cars back to the railroad so we could pick them up.

Now, this is mostly firsthand information as "Stuttering Bill" O'Brien and I took the pile driver out to Cisco on a work train that afternoon, and the next day Jim Bonnell and I were called for a work train to man the derrick at the wreck. We spent the following week picking up the pieces. That was my first working experience with a big wreck and I'm sorry to say it was not my last. Incidentally, it took 72 hours to drive a new temporary bridge and clear the line for service.

There was a touch of coincidence related to this derailment. It had been about ten years earlier when Jim Bonnell was firing the No. 1403 for my dad, once again during a period of rain, on an eastbound freight train. They came blasting through the Ruby Tunnel at full throttle and found Salt Creek in a roaring flood. Dad big holed the train and stopped just short of the washed out bridge. He swore you could not hear the whistle when he sounded a backup signal on account of the roar of the flood waters. He claimed that the rails ahead of his engine started to wash away as he backed off them. They spent the next couple of days in the siding at Ruby, waiting for a pile driver to set piles for a new span.

It was just east of that same Salt Creek wash out where George Cutting, on the No. 1605, hit a big rock and derailed his engine. George told me later how he got out of his seat on the right side and held on to the oil tray over the firebox door, and how brakeman Frank Pizza held on to him for dear life. Fireman Harold Dart got off the derailed locomotive and was struck and killed by some of the derailed cars behind the engine.

Another scene in the Price River Canyon of Utah in June 1917. Here the D&RGW grade was washed out west of Helper after the Schofield Dam failed. — S. A. DOUGHERTY COLLECTION

The yard and mainline was washed out at Castle Gate, Utah, also as a result of the Schofield Dam failure. While many of the bridges remained in tact, the approaches were washed out. — S. A. DOUGHERTY COLLECTION

Webster's International Dictionary defines a washout as: the washing away of earth especially in the bed of a railroad or a highway. The roadbed of the D&RGW in Utah was always subject to flashfloods, especially in the Wasatch Range and on the desert east of Helper. This accident is a result of high water in the Wasatch. The wreck is not identified as to time, place, train, or what locomotive it might be. — E. R. HOUSE COLLECTION

The 1400 class locomotives were built by Brooks in 1916 as Nos. 1250-1259. These engines were the only 2-10-2's or Santa Fe type power on the D&RGW. This class had the only cylindrical type tenders on the railroad. During World War II they were replaced with standard rectangular tenders. — R. H. KINDIG

It was a few years after that, over on the Salt Lake Division, when fireman Vance was killed in almost the same way. He was firing the No. 1408 for engineer Al Baxter. At 50 m.p.h. the engine broke a left side connecting rod and the piece that was still attached to the rear driver tore a hole in the front end of the mud ring, creating a boiler explosion-like effect. Fireman Vance unloaded at high speed and was killed by the fall, and after the train stopped the engineer got off and was found wandering around in a state of shock. The No. 1400-class engines were 2-10-2's, better known as the Santa Fe-type locomotive.

The explosion of a steam engine boiler was one of the most dreaded events that could happen on a railroad. It was nearly always fatal to head end crew members and devastating in its destruction. Imagine, if you will, the force that is generated when all of the water in the boiler, at the time of failure, turns to steam when released to atmospheric pressure. Let me tell you about the No. 1409.

36

It was during August 1934 and my mother, my youngest sister and I were returning from a trip to Los Angeles on the Union Pacific. Dad met our train in Salt Lake City; he was on the engineer's extra board at the time. We were in the old Rio Grande depot waiting for train Number Two to leave when the conductor came down stairs from the dispatcher's office and called dad over and whispered in his ear. Now the old man was a boomer hoghead and he had seen and heard a lot in his time, but he turned pale at whatever news he got. He came over where we were sitting and told my mother, "The No. 1409 blew up at Wellington and killed the crew on the engine. Engineer Harry Denman, fireman Joe Isherwood and brakeman Don Hendershott are dead."

Our train arrived in Helper around midnight and the next morning my Aunt Lola insisted on going to Wellington to see the wreck and take some pictures. She had known the victims from the Elks and the B of LF&E. Her first husband was old "Smokey" House. He had been killed in a sideswipe on the Southern Pacific at a place called Hayfed Siding near Sparks, Nevada. I know now that she had several very good reasons for taking young "Smokey" and me along. She no doubt surmised that we would one day hire out as firemen for the railroad and she wanted us to see first-hand what happens when a boiler explodes.

The 1400's, as already mentioned, were 2-10-2's with small drivers and developed 81,000 pounds tractive effort. They carried 195 p.s.i. working steam pressure and had 31x32-inch cylinders. They were old "Honest John" on a heavy grade, and an engineer could hardly get one to slip her wheels. The engines did have one serious drawback. They were equipped with a small, 8,000 gallon capacity Vanderbilt-type water tank, so naturally they were always hunting a drink. The locomotive was good for about one hour and ten minutes of hard work. Beyond that time, you had better be close to a tank or be ready to shake the fire to keep from burning the crown sheet. While these engines were assigned to the desert division they carried an auxiliary water car with an additional 8,000 gallons of water.

If you have never fired a steam locomotive you probably never heard of "bad water." Some railroad men never knew the meaning of the term, always having good, sweet, clear H_2O for use in their boilers. On the D&RG's desert division the water

The headlight and number plate of No. 1409 came to rest in the firebox following a boiler explosion which turned the chamber inside out. This accident took place on August 8, 1934, at Wellington, Utah. E. R. "Smokey" House is the young man on the left with his hands in his pockets. — E. R. HOUSE COLLECTION

The view at the left is the smoke box of the No. 1409 after the Wellington boiler explosion. (RIGHT) The combustion chamber of the 2-10-2 locomotive. — BOTH E. R. HOUSE COLLECTION

carried a lot of alkali, soluble and insoluble salts, and just plain mud. And gas . . . some kind of carbonation, that when it got hot and under pressure it would not make clean steam, just foam and froth. The carryover from the boiler washed away the lubrication from valves, pistons, cylinders, air pumps, water pumps and stoker engines. When one of those old hogs started to foam the engineer described the condition as "raising her water." The former sharp, clear exhaust from her stack began to sound like the engine was working oatmeal mush through the cylinders. And stink! Whew! It smelled of stale, dry dust, that which sticks in one's throat. Needless to say, a dry cylinder or valve soon lost its efficiency and the packing became shot and the piston began to leak steam. The worst result of foaming in the steam engine boiler was that you could not get an accurate reading of the water level from the sight glasses on the boiler head. The engineer never knew for certain how much water he might have in a foaming boiler. This is a dangerous condition, 'cause that firebox roof can get red-hot in a damn short time!

The fireman who could keep his engine from foaming had to carry the water level lower than normal working conditions might indicate and use the manual blowoff cock frequently. As the water evaporated the salts and silt settled to the bottom of the firebox mud ring, and this concentration was blown out into the atmosphere through the use of the blowoff cock. This manually operated valve was located in the locomotive cab, usually on the left side, under the fireman's seat, where it would be handy to use.

In the case of the No. 1409, the crew had stopped their westbound drag freight train at Green River, Utah, for coal, water, and to eat lunch. The coal chute man doped the rods and filled both water cisterns while the fireman straightened up his fire and the hoghead oiled around. Their next stop would be Woodside, 25 miles west. The train took around two hours en route to that water spout; then stopped to fill both tanks. The water supply for the Woodside tank was a deep well that had been drilled by the railroad in the early 1900's. Prior to drilling the well the D&RG ran a water train out from Helper daily; big wooden tubs mounted on flatcars and filled with pure, mountain spring water to supply the locomotives at that point. The water from the Price River was too full of alkali to use in steam boilers. The water

The tender of No. 1409 lies beside the auxiliary water car after the boiler explosion at Wellington, Utah, on August 8, 1934. (RIGHT) View of the derailed stock cars. — BOTH E. R. HOUSE COLLECTION

well was a gasser. Many years later it became famous as a tourist attraction, known as the "Woodside Geyser." It spouted about 15 or 20 feet high due to gas pressure.

For the crew of the ill-fated No. 1409, their next water tank stop was at Farnham. That tank was supplied from the river and was pumped out about where the wash from Desert Lake empties into that stream. The water in the wash runs deep green with a heavy concentration of salts. Now there is a mixture of carbonation and alkali salt in both tanks of the locomotive consist.

It was just about dark when the train topped the grade a mile west of Wellington and entered a little sag. The hoghead hooked her up and eased off on the throttle and "BLAM . . ." There was a horrible roar of an explosion and a bright, blinding flash!

The entire firebox tore away from the boiler and turned inside out, its heavy metal sheets ripped like so much paper, its stay bolts projecting like the quills of a giant porcupine; it flew to the right of the track and landed in the middle of U.S. Highway 50. The boiler and running gear remained on the rails and continued on west for a mile. It looked like a big tube mounted on wheels as the front end door had been blown off and had sailed like a huge plate, circular to the left across the river, where it came to rest in a field one hundred yards away. The Vanderbilt tank went up in the air and turned over, facing back toward the east, falling behind the auxiliary water car that once was trailing. The locomotive bell, which hung on the smokebox door was never found, or if it was, whomever found it kept it as a souvenir.

Examination of the left front boiler leg at the mud ring disclosed an area of about two square feet of rusty looking metal. It appeared that mud had settled there a foot deep, and then probably dried; there was no water circulation . . . so the metal got red-hot. The mudded space was burned, and it dried, the mud swelled and cracked open. When water poured into that void of heat and gas, the overheated metal cracked and the adjacent stay bolts failed. A tremendous explosion ripped the mighty Santa Fe-type asunder in one flashing instant.

A friend of mine, who was living in Helper and working on a track gang at Woodside that scorching day in August 1934, was riding on top of an empty stock car 15 cars deep from the head end of the train; about 750 feet behind the No. 1409. He had climbed aboard to ride home for the weekend. He told me later of his experience. He said that he was riding along, enjoying the cool evening breeze as he sat there on the running board of the swaying car, when suddenly there was a brilliant flash and a terrific roar such as he had never heard before, and he next found himself sitting in the willows along the river; the train was standing on the track nearby.

After viewing the wreckage and taking some pictures, Aunt Lola asked us to take her to the mortuary where the bodies of the victims were taken. Somehow she persuaded the mortician in charge to let us, as friends of the deceased, view their remains. I could describe in detail the damage inflicted on them. It was too horrible to relate. It was a lesson I'll never forget, and I'm sure now that my dear Aunty took us through this grisly experience as an object lesson in safety for budding firemen. You must watch the water level close, keep the boiler sweet, and don't let her foam. Also, the very first thing you do when you get on a steam engine is inspect the firebox, crown sheet and side sheets for burned areas. Always try the gauge cocks on the water column and blow out the water glasses. Get careless with the observation of these tenets and you could wind up under a sheet in the mortuary.

The next case of a boiler failure that I was involved in was when a big Mallet type engine, the No. 3703 blew up at Louviers,

Articulated No. 3703 blew up at Louviers, Colorado, on October 19, 1952, while en route from Denver to Pueblo. This is a view of the No. 2 engine of the blast-torn locomotive. — R. P. PARSONS COLLECTION

Four men died when the boiler of No. 3703 exploded at Louviers about 10:00 A.M. just south of Denver on the line to Colorado Springs and Pueblo. The locomotive was not dismantled until June of 1955. — R. P. PARSONS COLLECTION

Colorado, on October 19, 1952, killing four men. You can choose for yourself why it happened. Train No. 67 southbound, Denver to Pueblo, picked up a single unit diesel helper behind the crummy at Wolhurst . . . a running pickup no less. A few miles farther south as the big Baldwin built road engine, a 4-6-6-4, articulated, single expansion locomotive passed the Magazine Switch at the Hercules Plant her boiler exploded. The crew of three, along with a freelance photographer (who was reported as riding without permission) were all killed. The bright Sunday morning was shattered by a roaring boom that sounded as though the powder plant had exploded.

Upon viewing the crown sheet of the locomotive the next day it looked to me as if the metal had been overheated. Low water, or no water, in the area directly over the firebox had permitted it to burn. As long as you kept water on one side of that thick metal sheet you were safe. Let the crown sheet get dry and you've got trouble. It will get red-hot so quick it will make your head swim!

In this case, with an unauthorized passenger aboard, it might be safe to assume that the attention of the crew was distracted. Were they taking pictures, or talking picture taking, and in their suspected inattention allowing the water level in the boiler to get low? Then the water pump was started or increased in speed to feed more water into that red-hot area.

Since I was Road Foreman at the time, I accompanied the Big Hook from Pueblo the next day to the scene of the accident. We were all day loading the huge, ruptured boiler on a flatcar for its final trip to the scrap pile.

Shortly after the wreckage was brought in we made some tests with an identical type locomotive, using the feed water devices taken off the No. 3703 and put on the test engine. Using an identical train consist as to loads, empties and tons, and again with a single unit for a helper, we reproduced exactly the conditions that existed on the day of the explosion. There was no difficulty in supplying the boiler with water. Denver water was good, sweet, and nearly salt free, so foaming was not considered to be a factor in the tragedy.

Somewhere east of Kyune, Utah, on Soldier Summit, a light running 2-8-2 jumped the track. The date, incident, and cause of this odd accident are unknown. — E. R. HOUSE COLLECTION

The Colorado Midland operated for several years on a joint track with the D&RG between New Castle and Grand Junction, Colorado. The D&RG "Big Hook" holds up a CM 700-class locomotive at New Castle which was wrecked as a result of a derailment near Rifle. Date and details are lost to the sands of time. — JOHN B. NORWOOD COLLECTION

Locomotive No. 1184 on a work train in the Price River Canyon, above Lynn Siding, Utah, following washout trouble in 1917. Two dogs check out the pilot of the locomotive. Dogs are a familiar sight in many of the old rail snapshots.
— S. A. DOUGHERTY COLLECTION

45

An eastbound D&RG passenger train rolls through Ruby Canyon between Utaline and Shale, Colorado. This pictorial scene, photographed by Colorado photographer Louis C. McClure, was a standard view in early day D&RG pictorial literature. — DONALD DUKE COLLECTION

3

Joining The Birds!

THE EARLY 1920's were some bad years for the railroad on account of several passenger train wrecks. One of the earliest in my memory happened at Grassy Siding west of Woodside about five miles out on the Eastern Utah desert. It involved a double-header on train No. Two, the *Panoramic Limited*, an eastbound passenger schedule pulled by two Pacific-type 700-class locomotives. Fred Rader was one of the engineers involved.

I remember Rader as a tall, quiet man who wore a big, black hat. I was about five years old when he came to our house and it was his hat that impressed me most. Shortly after his visit to our place he was killed at Grassy. Our family rode a passenger train to Grand Junction to attend his funeral. I guess because we came from a pioneer railroad family and since grandma McComb ran a railroad beanery, all of her girls married railroad men. They knew everybody who worked out of Helper and were well acquainted with Fred Rader. He was a desert hogger who had enough seniority to hold a candy job (daylight passenger run) between Grand Junction and Helper.

The wreck of the "Palm Lily" on train No. 2, the *Panoramic Limited* at Grassy Siding, Utah, in 1922. — E. R. HOUSE COLLECTION

As our train passed the scene of the wreck two Big Hooks were engaged in picking up the "Palm Lily." That's what Rader called his pet locomotive. Engineers in those days took a great deal of pride in the machines under their care. Plenty of oil on their moving parts, careful inspection and lots of elbow grease on the brass trimming. The 700's had 72-inch driving wheels and were well known for their speed. They could really fly! They were still in service when I hired out and I had an opportunity to fire and run them for a few trips.

From the grown-up talk around the funeral I assumed that one of the engines had developed a hot pony truck; that is the leading wheel under the pilot or front end. The journal had failed just east of the east siding switch at Grassy and both engines turned over, along with several coaches. There were several passengers killed and many were injured, my memory fails to recall how many. The tall, gangling fireman in the cab with Rader was W.W. Gillies, who survived the crash with only minor injuries. I fired for "Bill" myself, many years after the accident happened, but he never

Requiem for engineer Fred Rader. Aunt Lola, shown in the black dress and broad brimmed hat, inspects the wreck of the "Palm Lily" at Grassy Siding, Utah, in 1922. — E. R. HOUSE COLLECTION

would open up and talk about it. The engineer on the second engine survived; however, his fireman was killed. The one bad feature of a steam engine was that in an upset, if it did not crush you to death in the cab, you could be sure of being scalded by the hot water and steam escaping from ruptured pipes.

The next real serious passenger train accident happened in September 1926. It involved the No. 1604 on train No. Two at a place called Waco on the Salida Division. The familiar words from the song *The Wreck of the Old 97,*

> They gave him his orders in Monroe, Virginy
> Saying, 'Pete, you're away behind time.
> This is not 38 but it's Old 97,
> You must put her in Lynchburg on time!

seems to have been written for engineer Hal Harpending and fireman Russel Willingham on that bright autumn Labor Day when they took the train out of Minturn, Colorado, with traveling engineer George Lillis riding along. As the story is told, it seems

Locomotive No. 1604, rests on her side in the Arkansas River after she jumped the track on Labor day of 1926, at Waco, Colorado. This accident is the result of excessive speed. The M-75 class 4-8-2 type was built by Baldwin in 1926. — R. P. PARSONS COLLECTION

that the crews had been having trouble making the running time on this schedule. Possibly the time was just too fast for the three percent grade to the top of the hill at Tennessee Pass and the numerous curves where the track follows the Arkansas River through Brown Canyon and the Royal Gorge en route to Pueblo. Certainly they had enough power from the giant Mountain-type 4-8-2 that the No. 1604 represented.

Traveling engineer Lillis was riding the train, we are told, to see why No. Two had been falling down on her schedule, and to exhort the crew to make the running time.

Well he turned and he said to his dirty, greasy fireman,
'Just shovel in a little more coal,
And when we cross that wide old mountain,
You can watch Old 97 roll!

No. Two had a helper out of Minturn and had to stop at Tennessee Pass to cut the Mikado-type off the head end. After

An injured passenger is being removed from one of the passenger cars at the Waco disaster. The wrecking crew watches from the bottomside of an overturned car, just waiting for the signal to begin the massive clean up once all the bodies are removed. — JOHN B. NORWOOD COLLECTION

Overall view of the Waco disaster, where No. 1604 jumped the track attempting to make a curve at high speed. — R. P. PARSONS COLLECTION (BELOW) The right-of-way is strewn with wrecked cars. Fortunately the coaches were of steel construction or more passengers might have been killed in this wreck. — JOHN B. NORWOOD COLLECTION

crossing "that wide old mountain" at 10,242 feet elevation, No. Two sailed along down the grade of the Arkansas and stopped at Malta for mail and passengers. Then streaked over the flats . . . Snowden, then Kobe where the rails enter the confines of a canyon west of Waco . . . The flanges were screaming against the shining rails as the big engine slipped in and out of the curves. This was Non-Automatic Block Signal Territory, and No. Two was a first class eastward train with right by class and direction over all trains. The engine crew did not know how fast they were rolling because there was no speed meter on the locomotive. They had the mile post markers, a standard watch and the seat of the hoghead's pants. A good engineer could judge the speed pretty close, if he paid attention. It was easy to tell from the way the engine took the curves . . . a smooth glide without side sway, or a jerking, slamming, with the cab snapping from side to side, and the flanges burning the rails. I can give the reader a pretty good description of the ride they got; I've been over this track a lot of times.

I knew "Rusty" Willingham and had ridden with him on both passenger and freight trains many times between Denver and Bond. He was a tall, rather quiet man with sandy hair and freckles. I also remember that he kept a very erect posture as a result of wearing a back brace, or corset which he had worn ever since he got out of the Salida Hospital back in 1926.

The M-75, 4-8-2-type were the largest of the big mountain jacks in use at the time. They were somewhat of an oddity in that they were three cylinder locomotives. The middle main rod was always a concern, although I never had one of them break on me. I used to think what a mess it would be if all of that jewelry between the drivers came apart while running. I fired and ran the No. 1604 many times in later years along with others of her class. They seemed a bit top-heavy and were restricted to 45 miles per hour when they were in service on the desert.

On that fatal day, as No. 1604 went speeding down the grade, "Rusty" got off his seat on the left side of the cab and crossed the deck to tell the engineer (his quote) "You had better set some air and slow this train. She'll never make the curve at Waco!" We can only imagine what the traveling engineer said, something to the effect that the fireman should go sit down, that the Superintendent

The Baldwin Locomotive Works delivered 10 of these 4-8-2's to the Denver & Rio Grande Western in 1926. The M-75 class had 67-inch drivers, three 25x30-inch cylinders, and produced 74,970 pounds of tractive effort. The middle cylinder was cast in the cylinder saddle on a cant to permit the rod clearance of the journal. — GERALD M. BEST

wanted No. Two in Salida on time. Now this fireman was a pretty old head to be holding a regular job on the varnish, and he had logged a lot of miles on this run. He was a damned good judge of speed, so he went to the left side gangway, slid down the handrails to the bottom step and got off at whatever speed they were running. That must have been one hell of a fall! But he lived. The others were not so fortunate.

He was found in the wreck with his hand on the throttle
And scalded to death by the steam.

As the speeding train entered the sharp curve at west Waco its locomotive left the rails in a great leap that carried it across the Arkansas River where it plowed a deep furrow in a gravel bar. Several coaches followed, upset, turned over, jammed and broke, and glass went flying. The engineer, the road foreman, and a deadhead engineer riding in the baggage car were killed. Also, many passengers were killed or injured and the equipment was badly damaged.

During my tenure as Trainmaster at Salida I worked with the Car Foreman, the derrick engineer and others of the crew that took the Big Hook to Waco to clear the line and pick up the mess. Thirty years after it happened they were still talking about their experience. Damaged cars and locomotives were picked up; some were repaired, others scrapped and forgotten. The trauma of passengers killed or injured lasts forever.

"Rusty" had two uncles who were engineers for the Rio Grande. I knew Uncle Danny who worked out of Salida; the other one I never met, but he gave me a hell of a scare one time. In 1941 I had a job painting aircraft for Consolidated in San Diego. One rainy February morning I was getting ready to leave for the plant when a radio newscaster told about an engineer on the D&RGW railroad being killed when his giant Mallet-type locomotive hit a huge boulder and turned over in the river. My father was still working out of Helper at the time, and I had cold chills at the vivid description of what happened until the announcer explained that the accident occurred in Gore Canyon in Colorado. A westbound freight going down grade through tunnel 35 hit a rock slide and derailed to the left side of the track, coming to rest in the river. The engineer in the cab was crushed; the fireman escaped by running back into the half empty coal tender. He was somewhat banged up, but survived. The "deadman" cables and chev are still buried under the grade near milepost 107. They used this arrangement of cables and pulleys, with a locomotive supplying power, to pull the great weight of the L-131 class 2-8-8-2 out of the chasm and onto the roadbed where the Big Hooks could get at it. Two derricks were required to set her back on her running gear.

Earl Roberts was one of the boys who worked as a hoghead on the Big Hill; he had been there a lot of years and had many exciting tales to tell of his experiences. He told me about the "ice train" runaway out of Pando. He was not reluctant to tell you of his part in the episode; telling on himself as a sort of humorous aside to the accident. He said he was firing a 3400-class Mallet for Herb Glessener out of Minturn way back when the company was still harvesting ice for the system icehouses. Every winter when the ice formed two feet thick on the lakes at Pando the company hired big gangs of winos to cut and store ice for summer use. It was the practice to call crews out of Minturn to haul the empty box

55

Locomotive No. 3406, a 2-8-8-2 Mallet articulated compound, is working hard on the two percent grade east of Arena, Colorado. This locomotive, built by Schenectady in 1913, provided the D&RGW with 38 years of faithful service before she was replaced by diesels. — R. H. KINDIG

cars and stock cars up the 12-mile three percent grade for ice loading. On this particular trip Roberts had worn a pair of brand new overalls, and he told me how they figured into this account.

It seems that the crew had turned their engine on the wye and then assembled the train of about 35 cars of ice. The air hoses were all coupled and the angle cocks opened. Or were they? Did the crew perform the required test of the air brakes? What really happened? The facts of the case are obscured by the passage of time. Earl said he was getting his engine ready to start down the grade, filling the boiler and building up his fire. In those days the engineer had to have a full boiler on level track so that when he pitched over on the three percent he would have water covering the crown sheet at the rear end of the long boiler.

One could hear the steel rails squeaking and popping in the sub-zero cold weather. At this point the elevation is around 9,000 feet and during the wintertime the temperatures get mighty low.

The big cylindered old hog waddled out through the switch to the main line and the train began to pick up speed. The hogger made an air brake application with the automatic brake valve and heard a sound most feared by all heavy grade hogheads. A short exhaust. . . . "pppfffttt." Low air. No air. . . however you say it, it is a condition of dread! The train was moving on a steep, descending grade with no brakes! At this point it is too late for analysis or recrimination. It is time to go "bird gang" or get the hell off! They were on a runaway! Earl said that he jumped from the right side gangway of the engine, feet first into the willows along the Eagle River. He landed in six feet of snow. When he had collected his wits, he tried to extricate himself from the hole he was standing in and walk back to the track. The train was naturally long gone. He found he could not move his legs! They were paralyzed, or broken; he could not move!

Glessner had jumped from the speeding engine soon after Roberts and the head brakeman had also unloaded. The conductor and rear brakeman had cut the caboose off the runaway and stopped it with the hand brake. I guess they figured there was no use compounding a mistake, so they took the safe course. All four came looking for Earl and when they found him, he was standing erect in the deep snow, unable to move his legs simply because the snow had packed inside the legs of his new overalls so tight there was no room for bending his knees!

The ice train sped on down the grade for another three miles until it left the rails and plowed into the depot at Red Cliff; where, we are told, the locomotive was so completely covered with ice and shattered cars that it could not be seen. A search was made for it west of Minturn. There were no injuries or fatalities involved in the wreck, only a great pile of scrap for the Big Hook to grapple. Wrecking in severe cold is a damned difficult chore, I can tell you from experience.

Not all of Earl Roberts' stories were as humorous as the one about the ice train runaway.

He told me about the time when he jumped from a "T-Model" 700-class engine into the icy waters of the Arkansas River near milepost 255, just before passenger trains No. 7 and No. 8 met head on in a grinding, awful crash around 2:00 P.M. on August 20, 1925.

The No. 3606 was pulling a long freight train eastward up the Eagle River grade toward Tennessee Pass. As the ponderous Mallet came around the eight degree curve west of Wolcott, Colorado, it struck a rock slide, derailed and rolled over into the rushing water. (TOP LEFT) In order to reach the derailed Mallet and bring her up, a spur track was built from the main line to the river's edge. Here two "Big Hooks" went to work on the 649,000 pound giant. (ABOVE) Looking like two long-necked vultures, the "Big Hooks" hover over the stricken locomotive. — ALL JOHN B. NORWOOD COLLECTION

Earl said he was firing for engineer R.T. Willingham on a helper engine, double-heading the westbound No. 7, which was the inferior train by timetable direction. Engineer Duncan and his fireman, Al Taughtenbaugh were on the second, or road engine in the hole. It is a long, uphill grade from Salida to the top of the hill at Tennessee Pass, and ten coaches was too much tonnage for one of those little high-wheel Pacifics to handle on the advertised.

The train dispatcher at Tennessee Pass had set up a meet between the two opposing first-class trains at Pine Creek (now called Princeton). With the double-header on No. 7 doing well, the dispatcher figured that they would be delayed unnecessarily at Pine Creek, so he put out a superceding order.

"No. 7 Engines 7-- and 7-- coupled meet No. 8 engine 778 at Granite instead of Pine Creek, etc. . . ."

No. 7 got their copy of the superceding order at Buena Vista, advancing their train four miles farther west of the original meeting point at Pine Creek to meet the eastbound varnish. No. 8 was to receive the notice of the change of meeting point from the operator at Malta, but for some unknown reason, No. 8's crew never got a copy of the critical order. Engineer J.A. Clare and fireman Phelan on the No. 778 on No. 8, went sailing by Granite, not knowing that No. 7 had been advanced beyond Pine Creek. When the poor train dispatcher learned that No. 8 had failed to get the notice of the change of instructions, he put out a call for a Big Hook at Salida, and called the hospital to alert them of an impending disaster. He knew that the lap of train order authority was sure to result in a "headlight" meet. There was no Automatic Block Signal System in use and all trains were operated by timetable authority.

Roberts told me that as the train passed Pine Creek he got down in the deck of his engine to put in a fire (all of the locomotives involved in this incident were hand fired). When he had finished shoveling he returned to his seat and looked back and waved to his friend, Al Taughtenbaugh on the second engine. As Earl turned to look up the track on the left-hand curve, he spied train No. 8 speeding down the 1.5 percent grade toward No. 7. He shouted a warning to engineer Willingham, ran to the gangway and leaped headlong into the fast flowing Arkansas. The engineer

This wreck is the result of two passenger trains meeting head-on while coming around a 12-degree curve. The accident was due to the failure of one train not receiving orders to stop at Granite. The death of an engine crew and the injury of 96 passengers resulted from this collision between the eastbound and westbound sections of the *Panoramic Limited*.

P. R. PARSONS COLLECTION

jumped from the right side cab window into the brush and rocks, breaking twelve ribs in the fall. Engineer Duncan also jumped in the nick of time but was not seriously injured. Fireman Al Taughtenbaugh was killed, crushed to death in the cab of his engine.

The engine crew on No. 8 did not see the westward train approaching in time to jump to safety. Engineer Clare was injured. His fireman, Phelan, was killed. The three Pacific-type locomotives were heavily damaged when the second engine on No. 7 climbed on top of the lead engine, collapsing the cistern and piling it on top of the boiler.

Engineer Tom Willingham was killed February 24, 1941 when the No. 3607 on train No. 41, *The Flying Ute*, hit a 20-ton rock in the Gore Canyon at Milepost 107, west of Kremmling, Colorado.

Fireman R.B. Willingham was firing for engineer Hal Harpending on No. 1604 on train No. 2, at 10:30 A.M. Labor Day, September 9, 1926 when 29 passengers, engineers Harpending,

View of the Granite head-on wreck from the bank of the Arkansas River. The double-header (westbound *Panoramic Limited*) is in the immediate foreground. Note the coach from the eastbound train nearly in the Arkansas River. — GERALD M. BEST COLLECTION

A jumble of iron and steel covers the right-of-way near Granite. The engine number of the westbound double-headed section of the train is not known nor was it reported in the Interstate Commerce Commission report. — GERALD M. BEST COLLECTION

An overall view of the Granite tragedy from high up on the west bank of the Arkansas River. Note how the coaches of the eastbound *Panoramic Limited* continued to roll past locomotive No. 778 after the impact.

— GERALD M. BEST COLLECTION

Here is a massive job for the Big Hook. Articulated No. 3600, a class L-131 2-8-8-2, is on her right side at Columbia Junction following a runaway on the Sunnyside Branch. — E. R. HOUSE COLLECTION

The Big Hook may be seen in the background, ready to lift No. 3600 and place it back on the rails following a 90 mile per hour runaway. — E. R. HOUSE COLLECTION

Gearhart, and traveling engineer George Lillis were all killed in the wreck at Waco. Gearhart was deadheading to Salida. The train speed was estimated to be around 50 m.p.h. when fireman Willingham got off, just before the locomotive and six coaches overturned in the river.

Many spectacular runaways have occurred on the heavy grades of the Rio Grande branch lines. Two of these unfortunate accidents stand out in my mind mainly because, even though a great deal of damage resulted, no one was injured. Both accidents were caused by an apparent failure to comply with air brake rules and good train handling practice.

The Sunnyside Branch was built in the early 1900's to service the coal mines and coke ovens that were developed in the Range Creek area of the Book Cliffs. The ruling grade from Mounds Junction to the mines was four percent ascending, and increasing to about six percent above the town where the line extended to the Utah Rock Asphalt operation. It was no place to fool around with air brakes. All cars left standing had to have a hand brake set full wrap. The air brake system on all trains had to be fully charged *before* letting off the hand brakes on long trains or cuts of cars. Standard air brake tests were required for all trains before departing Sunnyside. Retainer valves were also placed in the heavy holding position (20 pounds) at that point.

The crew of the ill-fated No. 3600 West assembled their coal train in the predawn hours of a frigid morning in February. The winds out of the canyon were right off the ice floes of the Arctic, and sometimes under these conditions, the crews would take shortcuts while making the necessary tests. That might be what happened in this case.

The engineer in charge of the No. 3600 was a young runner, and he did not have much experience on such a heavy grade, so it may be that his train crew led him down the primrose path to destruction by releasing all of the hand brakes before he had a chance to charge his train air brakes. Before he could release the independent brake on the engine, the slack ran in and the train started down hill fast. With the full weight of 60 loads of coal kicking him in the rear, away he went! He made a light application, but it did not check his speed. Then the inexperienced hogger made an emergency application all at once, but for some

Twisted iron and splintered wood of wrecked coal cars mark the path of the Sunnyside Branch runaway. Just cleaning up the dumped coal on the ground and in the cars made for an enormous undertaking. — E. R. HOUSE COLLECTION

unknown reason it was not effective. As the speed increased the trainmen got off and left the engineer and his fireman alone on the runaway.

An eyewitness, working on a project near the track, saw the train pass out of control. He later swore that the speed was around 90 m.p.h.! Much too fast to unload, so the engine crew rode it out!

At Columbia Junction a five degree curve at the west end of the yard marked the end of their terrified flight. The big L-131-class 2-8-8-2 turned over on her left side, her engineer and fireman still in the cab holding on for dear life, while she slid for about a hundred yards down the Junction Yard tracks. The train of coal piled in great heaps of junk behind her. A diesel yard switcher off the United States Steel mine run was parked on one of the tracks and it was struck and damaged by the derailed equipment. No one was injured, thank God.

Who goofed? Or was it a frozen brake pipe? Were all of the angle cocks open, and were all of the air hoses coupled? Was it a failure to charge the train air pressure to the proper level before releasing the hand brakes? The use of all car retaining valves was required for safe operation on this branch, however, it is a moot question if the auxiliary reservoirs are not properly charged.

In the case of another runaway on the Spring Canyon Branch, which is also a heavy grade operation of about 4.5 percent, a crew coming down the hill with a big train of coal stopped at the Junction Yard to knock down the "pops" (car retaining valves). While the two brakemen were going over the standing train, the hogger had to attend to a hurried call of nature in a nearby tavern. Later his fireman became worried about his absence and went to look for him. Meanwhile, with the last retainer down, the brake cylinder pressure on each car released to atmosphere, the train slack ran in against the L-62, a 2-6-6-2 type No. 3300 and away it went! A passing motorist ran into the bar to tell the startled engine crew that their train had gone off without them. As the runaway reached the main track at Helper it sideswiped an eastbound freight train that was pulling in the yard. The escapee turned over and rolled down the embankment and ended up in a hay field beside the Price River.

Denver & Rio Grande Western's No. 3615, one of the largest articulated locomotives on the road, by weight and tractive effort, assists No. 1804 (4-8-4) on train No. 2, the *Scenic Limited*. On this bright October day in 1939, the train consisted of 14 cars and both locomotives were working hard on the three percent grade west of Mitchell, Colorado. — R. H. KINDIG

4

An Old Superstition

T*HERE IS* an ancient myth about railroad wrecks occurring in series of three. I never believed that fable
because, where does one begin to count, or where do you
stop? What interval of time passes between major derailments?
There are periods of time, however, where the accident frequency
within a short time span would tend to support such a theory. Like
October 1941, for example.

As I recall there was a bad wreck at Colton, Utah on October 6th
or 7th of that year. It was just one week before the No. 1601 on
First No. 38 went through the washout at Cisco where Murphy
was killed. The Colton affair involved *The Flying Ute*, a hotshot
westbound freight with two big Mallets double-heading, and a
light engine off a previous helping assignment. I have some
pictures of the mess. Three giant articulated locomotives were
torn to pieces, turned over, bent, twisted; a huge pile of scrap. The
Ute was making 40 m.p.h. around the curve at the east Colton
crossover. Fireman J.W. Hammond on the No. 3509, the leading
Mallet, lost his right leg below the knee when they slammed into
the light engine standing on the crossover. It was a miracle that
no one was killed or others injured. It was lucky for Hammond

Locomotive Nos. 3509 and 3709 were highballing the *Flying Ute*, a westbound fast freight, when they struck a light engine trying to make an east crossover at Colton, Utah, in October 1941. Big Hook No. 025 is about to roll No. 3509, the lead engine of the *Ute*, back on the track.
— JOHN CRAWFORD

that one of the brakemen was wearing a necktie, which they used as a tourniquet on Jim's leg to stop the bleeding.

As a result of the emergency first aid given, and using the only material available, one of the firemen working out of Grand Junction (me) requested that first aid kits should be installed and maintained on all locomotives and cabooses. Hell, the next brakeman might not be a natty dresser, and someone could bleed to death for lack of a cravat. The company readily agreed to our request and first aid material has been furnished ever since.

Operating Rule No. 104 in the 1938 issue of the Rules and Regulations of the Operating Department reads in part as follows:

"When a train or engine is waiting to cross from one track to another and during the approach or passage of a train on tracks involved, all switches connected with the movement must be secured in the normal position. Before starting to make the movement, all switches involved must be properly lined and not restored to normal until the movement is completed."

Three giant articulated locomotives were torn to pieces, turned over, bent, twisted: a huge pile of scrap. Believe it or not, all three locomotives were rebuilt in the D&RGW's Burnham Shops in Denver. — JOHN CRAWFORD

In part, Rule 513, third paragraph, reads as follows:

"Both switches of a crossover must be open before a train or engine starts to make a crossover movement and the movement must be completed before either switch is restored to normal position."

Operating rules must provide the fullest measure of protection for employees and the rules must be constantly revised to meet safety and service requirements. In the 1948 reissue Rule 513 had a new fourth paragraph that read:

"Unless otherwise provided, before a train or engine enters or fouls a main track, or crosses from one main track to another, it must wait three minutes after any switch or derail connected with the movement has been operated to effect a signal indication."

A better understanding of the rules and strict compliance with their requirements by the employees involved would, no doubt, have prevented this pileup and serious personal injury. You see, that light engine was occupying the crossover, waiting for the fireman to line the switches ahead of its movement. The locomotive should have remained in the clear of the main track until *all* of the crossover switches were properly lined. In that manner the locomotive could have made a continuous movement to the eastward main track, after which, the fireman would restore all switches to their normal position.

My old man gave me a lot of good advice, mostly about working for the railroad. Some of the best was regarding the Operating Rules. "You learn 'em, and you live up to 'em. Never try to substitute your own wants or wishes. Use all of your experience and knowledge to sustain the rules, not to supplant or circumvent them." He used to say that a little rules violation was like a little pregnancy . . . it was bound to get worse. He tried to work according to his own advice, too. He had an excellent record of no demerits or dismissals, and with no serious accidents or injuries.

There was another instance back during the early part of World War II, where two train derailments occurred within the same week. That was when the No. 1705 and her sister M-64 the No. 1706 each overturned and their engineers were killed. One happened on the Salt Lake Division at Scenic, just west of Soldier Summit and the other at Eagle, over on the old Grand Junction Division. In each case the locomotives were pulling passenger trains, and in each derailment only the locomotives were involved. There were no coaches damaged and no passengers killed or injured.

In the case of the Scenic wreck, old No. 5, the westbound *Exposition Flyer* would get a helper on the point out of Helper. The procedure called for the inbound hogger to set the air on his train and make a water spout stop, then cut out his brake valve. After the hostler had coupled the helping engine to the train, the engineer on the lead locomotive would cut in his automatic brake valve. He would wait for a signal from the carmen to release and recharge the train line, and then made a set and release in order to test the brake operation from his valve. After the blue flag was removed he waited for a sign from the ORC (Conductor). When he got the "highball" he answered with two blasts of the whistle, placed the "Johnson Bar" (reverse lever) in full forward position, released the independent brake on his engine and eased out on the

The No. 1705, after cutting off her helper at Soldier Summit, works the *Exposition Flyer* down the grade. All of a sudden there was no air. The No. 1705 jumped the tracks at Scenic and landed on her side. — JOHN B. NORWOOD

The derailed *Exposition Flyer*, train No. 5, at Scenic. The engine broke away from the lead baggage car, leaving the track and sliding down the hill. The Big Hook is in the background, ready to pull the baggage car and No. 1705 up the slope. — JOHN B. NORWOOD

Leaving Minturn and moving west, Extra No. 1706, rolled down the long sustained grade and through the curves along the Eagle River. Suddenly No. 1706 jumped the tracks killing engineer D. C. Cornwall. — E. R. HOUSE COLLECTION

steam throttle. The train moved forward slowly as he gave her a little more steam. He hooked her up on the quadrant and opened the throttle wide as the speed increased. The staccato exhaust of the two big jacks filled the canyon with sound. Next a running air test was made, and an automatic brake reduction brought about an air whistle from the engine cab signal, indicating that the rear brake had been applied, and two more toots to signal a release.

At the summit the hoghead on the helper made a service reduction to stop the train. As the speed decreased his fireman would drop off the engine, close the brake pipe angle cock, lift the coupler cutoff lever and signal the engineer to take off down the main line with the fireboy clinging to the rear tank step. After passing the trailing crossover switch the fireman then dropped off and lined the "gate" (switch) and gave his hogger a backup signal to move back in the clear on the passing siding. During this operation the road engineer cut in his brake valve doubleheading cock and recharged the train air system. He made a set and release of the brakes and as soon as the helper engine got clear of the main "high iron" he whistled off. When he received a signal from his crew, the engineer made a running air test as the train departed the summit to enter the descending grade. So far so good.

The sleek passenger train accelerated smoothly and swiftly on the heavy downgrade. The engineer now set the air to check his train speed. Nothing happened! What went wrong? What had been overlooked or ignored? About three miles farther west the locomotive left the rails, breaking away from the lead baggage car, and rolling over the steep embankment, plowing through snow covered rocks and oak brush. The engineer was killed; the fireman scrambled from the wreckage of his engine and climbed back to the track where he met the other crew members to tell them of the fate of the unfortunate engineman. How the fireman survived the terrible crash only the Good Lord knows! Two baggage cars left the rails, no passengers were hurt, and no track was damaged. How can one account for this miracle?

How can anyone account for the second, almost identical upset at Eagle within the same week?

During World War II troop trains were numerous. Soldiers, sailors and all branches of the service were transported in passenger coaches designated as "Main" trains. It was common to run several sections of a first-class train schedule in order to move the great flood of men and women going to war, or to run these special trains as extras with right over all trains.

Such a "Main" train departed Minturn moving west, down the long sustained grade through the curves along the Eagle River. East of the siding called Eagle a three mile tangent precedes a sharp curve just east of the east siding switch. The straight track was an invitation for some engineers to pick up a little time by speeding over the straightaway and relying on a heavy brake reduction to slow for the restricted curve. As the locomotive on this train entered the curve the train crew felt a lurch and the train brakes applied in emergency. Looking out the windows on the right side of the coach they saw a big cloud of dust and recognized that their engine had broken off the head end and turned over on the right side of the track, where it came to rest behind the wooden water tank! The train rolled on to a stop in front of the station. The engineer was killed, but the fireman escaped serious injury. There were no other injuries, nor damage to track or equipment. How can things like this be explained? Well, certainly the train speed exceeded the maximum overturning speed for the curve. The engine crew were experienced men. Was this a case of flagrant rule violation governing permissable speed? Did the engineer go to sleep? Or had he been drinking before going on duty? There are many unanswered questions about the two accidents that were almost identical as to their cause and end results.

Dead men answer no inquiry. Sometimes even the living are reluctant to tell what really happend.

Some time later there was a near-miss at Eagle involving a light engine west; in charge were only an engineer and a fireman. It was called to go to Funston, turn, and then help an eastbound freight from that point east to Minturn. Their adversary in this case was a freight drag east. The extra east had right over the light engine west with a string of train order waiting points and specified times, but the engine crew of extra west figured they had time to run to Ortega Siding before the superior train arrived. The hoghead stopped his engine at the east switch to permit his fireman to line their move into the siding to clear for the eastbound train. It was customary, as the rule required, to pull in the clear of the main line to let the fireman line the switch back to normal position. Then he would run up to the standing engine, get aboard, and the engine then pulled up once again and stopped 600 feet from the west siding switch to wait in the clear for the opposing train. Only in this case, after entering the passing siding, the engineer failed to stop! The movement continued on slowly westward with the poor fireman running behind, trying to catch his engine! No way . . . out the west end . . . running through the siding switch points and off, away toward the west, leaving the fireboy behind.

The eastbound train proceeded on its way, smoking up the grade, and coming at them was a big L-131 class Mallet, with no indication of what had happened at Ortega! When the train was closely approaching the east switch at Eagle, the green ABS (Automatic Block Signal) governing their movement went red in their face. STOP! The train head end brakeman was very alert, and he got off with his flagging kit and ran toward the east siding switch. There was a headlight coming. "Hell, he sure is on our time. Where in hell does he think he's going?" He lined the switch for the passing track to let the Mallet enter. Whew! Some relief, but Jesus, he still ain't gonna stop! And where was the fireman? He should have been on the left side in the cab when the No. 3600 headed in . . . at least to say thanks. Those jerks!

There is a sag in the track toward the west end of the Eagle Siding; the big engine, now low on steam pressure on account of no fireman on board to keep her hot, stopped in the sag. The air pump stopped for lack of steam and the brakes applied. The runaway was safe.

What had happened to that hoghead? Was it a stroke? An epileptic seizure, or did he go to sleep? Had he been using alcohol or drugs? There was a formal investigation held and the man was dismissed for his responsibility in connection with his alleged failure to comply with the Rules and Regulations of the Operating Department, specifically rules 10-A, Red ABS, stop signs given frantically by his deserted fireman. Rules S-72, S-78, S-87, 104, 106, 507, 509-A, etc. etc. Thank God there was only a damaged west switch at Ortega Siding. Except for an alert head brakeman doing his job, there would have been a head-on collision.

A little further on I'll tell you about a couple of head-on crashes that produced some disastrous results.

Sometime, when you recall the old myth about accidents happening in series of three's, consider the experience of a fireman I know who had a succession of three misfortunes within a short span of time. In each instance he lost his pocket watch. The first incident, of the trio, was the wreck of the No. 1705 on train No. 5 west of Soldier Summit where his engineer was killed. In the second accident, he was the fireman working on a four-unit diesel consist that was involved in a head-on collision near Gomex, at the mouth of Spanish Fork Canyon in Utah. That portion of the railroad was two main tracks, or "double-track" territory from Provo to Helper over the Wasatch Range. On this particular day a section of the two main tracks was being used as single track, under the provisions of the old rule D-513, while some major repair work was in progress. The section of track affected was between two crossovers. A train crew, consisting of a conductor and two brakemen, was called to provide flag protection as required by rule 99 on the single track. One brakeman was at

77

By the time diesel locomotives came on the scene, accidents on the Denver & Rio Grande Western, resulting solely from the misreading or disregard of the timetable, were rare. Head-on crashes were more likely to arise due to errors in the train order/dispatching system. Dispatcher's error resulted in the head-on collision of two diesel powered freight trains at Gomex, Utah, in 1943. In this case, No. 542 westbound met the No. 550 eastbound and thus the first accident on the road to involve diesel locomotives. In the views on the opposite page, the reader may see the jackknifed units. (ABOVE) The "Big Hook" is attempting to place the No. 542 back on the track. The No. 1403 steam locomotive, complete with Vanderbilt tender, is working the wrecking train. — ALL JOHN B. NORWOOD COLLECTION

the west crossover, while the conductor and the other man were at the east crossover. The crew was in telephone communication with the train dispatcher and were to handle, through him, what traffic he wanted to move in preference over the track that was still in service.

As the saga unfolds, one brakeman at the west crossover got on the phone and called Ds (train dispatcher).

"I've got a diesel here to go east."

"Ok, let him come."

And shortly thereafter, the brakeman at the east crossover came on the line.

"Hey, dispatch', I've got a diesel here . . ."

"Let him come, I told you."

So, it was another job for the Big Hook. The two trains met at about 25 miles per hour. The No. 550 tried to climb over the top of the No. 542. One engineer suffered a broken ankle; a diesel maintainer friend of mine also broke his ankle when he leaped to safety just before the crash. The fireman who lost his timepiece had remained in his seat on the engine until someone got up in the cab and asked him if he was hurt.

"No," he said, "I'm just too scared to move."

That was the first, big, bad pileup which involved diesel locomotives on the Rio Grande.

As a result of that snafu, a new provision was added to Rule D-153. Called the Pilot Block Rule, it required that all traffic be handled under the direction of the conductor who was stationed at the location of the single-track, and he would be required to ride each train movement over the portion of railroad being used as single-track. While the pilot rode through the block, his brakemen flagged and held all traffic.

A short time later, this same fireman was promoted to engineer, and was running north of Salt Lake, when his locomotive sideswiped a southbound freight at Woods Cross during a period of dense fog. He lost his third watch in that accident. It was told around the sandhouse that the unfortunate hogger went to the Division Superintendent and asked him if the company made any provision for replacing watches lost in accidents. Sorry . . . they did not.

Let us go way, way back, say to 1908. It must have been around

80

This is the result, of the sixth section, of an Elks Club (BPOE) special train not carrying green to indicate another section of the train was following. Engine No. 1189, on an eastbound stock train, pulled out of the siding and into the path of the seventh section and a head-on collision at Whitehouse, Utah in May of 1908. — S. A. DOUGHERTY COLLECTION

that time because the C-48 class, Consolidation-type, numbered 1100 through the 1198 came during that period of 1906-1908. The old picture of the wreck shows the No. 1189 on an eastward livestock train tangled with the locomotive of a westbound passenger special. The smoke box of the No. 1189 is telescoped into the front end of the other engine. She has a shattered stock car riding piggyback on the cistern. The westbound engine has a wooden coach, split open, riding on her tank. There were many fatalities; both passengers and crew members died, not to mention a great number of sheep. The crash occurred between Whitehouse and Elba. If you have ever been across this remote stretch of desert you know how wild and desolate it is. A place best described as where the jack rabbits carry their lunch.

As history relates the events of that black day there were seven, BPOE, Elk Specials west, all running as sections of a regular

schedule. Only there must have been some mix-up, because
Section Number 6 went by Elba displaying no green flags or
green lights on the front of his engine to indicate to opposing
trains that there was a following section running on the same
schedule and having the same superiority, or precedence as the
six leading trains. The hoghead on the eastward sheep train, in
the siding at Elba to meet the fleet of passenger trains, told his
head shack to line the switch for the main track. He headed out
and started down the main. From the impact of the collision as
evidenced by the destruction shown in the photograph, he had
gained considerable momentum through the Whitehouse sag
when around the right hand curve came the seventh section of the
opposing passenger train fleet! The two trains met head on. I

This photograph shows the intensity of the wreck of No. 1189, an eastbound stock train, after it tangled with the locomotive of the seventh section on the westbound BPOE special at Whitehouse, Utah. — s. a. DOUGHERTY COLLECTION

visited the scene of the crash many years later and picked up shards of broken porcelain from the wrecked diner of that Elk Special.

Those old pictures held quite a fascination for a wide-eyed kid. I can't tell you how many times I looked at them. In later years, as I came swinging around that same curve on a speeding train, I gave thought to the men who died in that smashing collison, and thanked heaven for the signal system in use when I worked across the desert.

A rock slide is, of course, difficult for enginemen to see when traveling at any speed on a twisting mountain railroad. The No. 3601 hit a rock slide in Debeque Canyon, Colorado, between Rifle and Palisade in 1926. The locomotive was rerailed and here she is with the "Big Hook" at Akin.
—JOHN B. NORWOOD COLLECTION

A derailment may be caused by a dragging part, a burned off journal, a broken wheel, an obstruction on the track, a broken rail, or any number of things. The "Big Hook" at Helper, Utah, was called out to clean up the mess shown in these two views. The No. 3701 was used to handle the wrecking train. — BOTH JOHN B. NORWOOD COLLECTION

It became my unhappy duty one time as a Road Foreman to take the Big Hook, the No. 027, out of Salida on a chilly November day to the scene of another head-on collision at a siding called Dos on the old Grand Junction Division. There were two engineers killed on that early morning as passenger train No. 19 westbound met a Denver bound freight train head on just east of the east switch at Dos.

The accident happened in CTC (Centralized Traffic Control) territory, single-track under the remote control of the train dispatcher from his central office in Grand Junction. In a CTC System there is no superiority of trains established by timetable or by train orders. Precedence is conveyed by signal aspect. All positive signals are under the control of the dispatcher. Dual-controlled switches are lined for movements in and out of the sidings, and the necessary information is displayed by trackside signals. Train handling, such as starting, stopping and speed control are accomplished by the individual hoghead on each train as indicated by the aspect of the signals governing his movement.

Now we are advanced into the age of diesels where firemen no longer shovel coal or shake grates or bog ashes; the trainmen no longer get off and run ahead to line the switches. The trains are longer and heavier, and the speeds are higher, but the engineman has the same responsibility to control his train or locomotive speed as he did on the old steam engines.

If my memory serves me well, No. 19 got a yellow intermediate block west of Lacy Siding, "Proceed at medium speed, approach the next ABS (Automatic Block Signal) prepared to stop. Trains exceeding 30 miles per hour must at once reduce to that speed." The engineer and fireman acknowledged the signal aspect and reduced to the required speed and continued on toward Dos. When their locomotive topped the rise east of the siding they were able to see the next ABS down a long tangent . . . "Red-over-yellow." The top light governs the main track. The lower light governs the turnout. The timetable indicated a 30 mile per hour switch. "We're gonna take the hole for some lousy freight drag east." The dialogue is familiar. "Oh, well, we are on time, and with this little, short train we can duck right in, go through the pass and make the dispatch' happy with a nonstopper."

Only that was not to happen. As No. 19 approached the east

86

switch they could see the bright headlight at the front end of the eastward train coming at them down the main . . . "Why don't that moron dim that damn light?" About that time the ABS governing the passenger train went red in their face! The freight drag had run by the stop signal that governed its movement! Hell, it had to be red. The switch was lined for No. 19 to enter the siding.

The head brakeman of the Denver bound train was standing in the open doorway on the left side of the cab; he leaped to safety just before the rending crash of the two giant locomotives. The freight train fireman was back in the trailing cab, and neither man was hurt. When the speeding monsters met east of the switch the Alco No. 6000 on Train No. 19 reared upright and toppled to the right, or north side of the track, killing its engineer; the fireman suffered a broken neck. The big Electro-Motive unit on the freight drag rose full height and plunged over the embankment on the south side, also killing the man in the right side seat of her cab.

It was a cold, miserable three days that followed as we picked up the wreckage. All derailments are bad, but with fatalities, they are unspeakable. There is a funeral-like atmosphere reflected by everyone engaged in the clean up. For days after you get the Hook back in the barn thoughts of what happened keep running through your head and you keep asking why? Human error? Sleep, booze, drugs? There has to be an answer. No man in his right mind, alert, sober or conscious can run his locomotive by a red signal and into the bright beam of that early morning headlight, knowing as all engineers must, the ultimate result.

The Big Hook stationed at Helper, Utah, assists with the removal of the old turntable, at the pit, just outside the Helper roundhouse. — S. A. DOUGHERTY COLLECTION

5

The Wrecking Crew and Equipment

FROM WHAT has been said up to this time you might have conceived the idea that the Road Foreman of Engines was the only one in supervision who was required to go to major derailments. That is not so. He is one of many, but the one whom management relies on most to be available to accompany the Big Hook to the scene of an accident. At the terminal it is his duty to make a check of the locomotive and the crew that is called for the derrick; he supervises the air test and tries to get the outfit out of the yard without delay. The main line may be tied up, or worse, there could be employees trapped in the wreckage. Every second counts, so expedite the movement. On arrival at the wreck scene he supervises switching the Hook to the head end and to get her up to where the work is, and if necessary he relieves the engineer at meal time, etc. The Road Foreman works with the Chief Dispatcher to line up movements of other trains as soon as the line is open. He must stay with the derrick through the picking up, rerailing, rebuilding and the assembly of the "hospital train," and then ride along with the wrecked equipment back to the home terminal. It may take a few hours or several days. On some of the most extensive wrecks, determined by the number of cars and units involved, the location, and the weather, I have been out for five days at one stretch!

The others required to attend these affairs are the Division Superintendent or his assistant, the Trainmaster, the Roadmaster, Chief Engineer and the Claim Department representative, as well as, Special Agents and the Superintendent of Safety, Rules and Training. The Mechanical Department is well represented by the General Car Foreman, Chief Mechanical Officer and the Master Mechanic. If this looks like all Chiefs and no Indians, guess again. They all have plenty to do.

There are the section gang foremen and their men who remove the damaged rails and ties and then rebuild the track. The derrick foreman and his men handle the blocks, hooks and slings used in picking up and retrucking the battered cars and locomotives. These men are the unsung heroes; the first to arrive and the last to leave the scene of trouble. They work hard from early to late and then start again. In one instance, which I'll tell you more about later, the wrecking crew worked for 23 hours to bring one F-9 EMD unit out of the Colorado River bottom up to grade level and rerail it, the gang only stopping to let traffic through and to grab a bite to eat.

As the reader might suppose, the Rio Grande crews were experts in the wrecking business. They got a lot of practice and were some of the world's best, with no exceptions, at no time, and at no place! There are two who stand out in my memory. G.S.D. "Jerry" McCall was a Trainmaster off the old Denver & Salt Lake Railroad (Moffat Route) who got his training in the school of hard knocks. He could do more with rerailing frogs and a few well placed blocks than any man I ever saw; more than most men could do with a derrick. Ever see a jammed coupler freed with dynamite? He could do anything around a wreck that needed to be done, from setting blocks and frogs to skinning a "cat." And if one thing he tried didn't work he was never without an alternative plan of action that would.

Right along with McCall, at the top, was C.L. "Swede" Olson, the system General Car Department Foreman. I've never seen a harder worker and he knew his stuff! On some of the real bad derailments he would work around the clock and do more than three men.

The derricks were numbered 022 through 029 and had a 150-ton lift capacity. Originally they had coal fired steam boilers to furnish power. Later they were converted to fuel oil, and eventually the steam gave way to diesel engines. The machines were powerful as hell, but very restricted as to their capabilities . . . having only a 56½-inch base (the width of the track). They were inclined to be top-heavy, and while they had a 360 degree swing, you could not make much of a lift at anything over 12 degrees of center. The largest one in service was old "Sampson de Grande," so named in a company sponsored contest to select a fitting cognomen for this monster. To make a heavy lift, you first set blocks alongside the machine fore and aft just outside the rails on the ends of the ties and then jacked the outriggers in position over the blocks. "Armstrong" (manual) was the power used to move these babies before hydraulic or compressed air was adopted. Next wedges were set to shim the riggers. Rail clamps front and rear were fastened to keep the force applied at the boom end from raising the rear end off the rails. With the long boom at one end and the machinery house at the other, you had to have plenty of side clearance or go "endo" with this old boy. And if you were on a curve that had much elevation and you wanted to turn end for

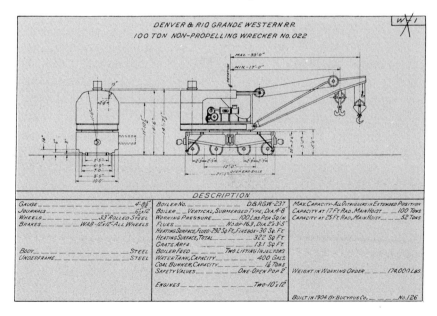

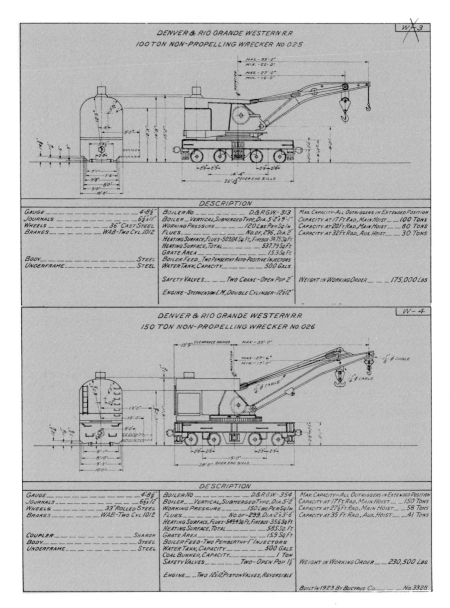

DENVER & RIO GRANDE WESTERN R.R.
100 TON NON-PROPELLING WRECKER No. 025

DESCRIPTION

GAUGE	4-8½	BOILER No.	D.&R.G.W.-313
JOURNALS	6½×11	BOILER–VERTICAL, SUBMERGED TYPE, DIA. 5'2½-9'-1"	
WHEELS	36" CAST STEEL	WORKING PRESSURE	120 LBS. PER SQ. IN.
BRAKES	WAB–TWO CYL. 10/12	FLUES	No. of, 296, DIA. 2"
		HEATING SURFACE, FLUES–503.04 SQ. FT., FIREBOX 34.75 SQ. FT.	
		HEATING SURFACE, TOTAL	537.79 SQ. FT.
BODY	STEEL	GRATE AREA	15.3 SQ. FT.
UNDERFRAME	STEEL	BOILER FEED–TWO PEMBERTHY AUTO-POSITIVE INJECTORS	
		WATER TANK, CAPACITY	500 GALS.
		SAFETY VALVES	TWO CRANE–OPEN POP 2"
		ENGINE–STEPHENSON L.M., DOUBLE CYLINDER–12×12"	

MAX. CAPACITY–ALL OUTRIGGERS IN EXTENDED POSITION	
CAPACITY AT 17 FT. RAD., MAIN HOIST	100 TONS
CAPACITY AT 20 FT. RAD. MAIN HOIST	80 TONS
CAPACITY AT 32 FT. RAD. AUX. HOIST	30 TONS
WEIGHT IN WORKING ORDER	175,000 LBS.

DENVER & RIO GRANDE WESTERN R.R.
150 TON NON-PROPELLING WRECKER No. 026

DESCRIPTION

GAUGE	4-8½	BOILER No.	D.&R.G.W.-354
JOURNALS	6½×12	BOILER–VERTICAL, SUBMERGED TYPE, DIA. 5'-2"	
WHEELS	33" ROLLED STEEL	WORKING PRESSURE	150 LBS. PER SQ. IN.
BRAKES	WAB–TWO CYL. 10/12	FLUES	No. of–299, DIA. 2½'-3'-6"
		HEATING SURFACE, FLUES–549.1 SQ. FT., FIREBOX–35.6 SQ. FT.	
		HEATING SURFACE, TOTAL	585 SQ. FT.
COUPLER	SHARON	GRATE AREA	15.9 SQ. FT.
BODY	STEEL	BOILER FEED–TWO PEMBERTHY–I" INJECTORS	
UNDERFRAME	STEEL	WATER TANK, CAPACITY	500 GALS.
		COAL BUNKER, CAPACITY	1 TON
		SAFETY VALVES	TWO–OPEN POP 1½"
		ENGINE	TWO 12×12, PISTON VALVES, REVERSIBLE

MAX. CAPACITY–ALL OUTRIGGERS IN EXTENDED POSITION	
CAPACITY AT 17 FT. RAD., MAIN HOIST	150 TONS
CAPACITY AT 27½ FT. RAD., MAIN HOIST	58 TONS
CAPACITY AT 35 FT. RAD., AUX. HOIST	41 TONS
WEIGHT IN WORKING ORDER	230,500 LBS.
BUILT IN 1923 BY BUCYRUS CO.	No. 3328

end, or just at right angles, forget it! You had to move back to some flat tangent or you would tip the damn thing over.

The derricks had a single boom with two hooks, each on a separate line. The little hook was for lifting small stuff such as a pair of wheels in a frame (called a truck), a coupler, or a light load.

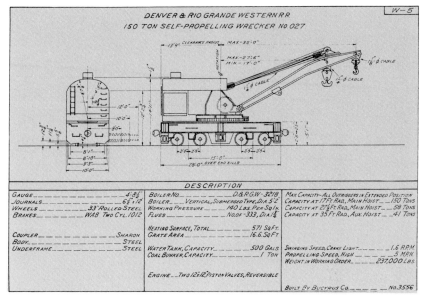

For lifting locomotives or heavy loads, the big hook was used. The hook itself was never attached to the object being lifted. You always used a chain, a sling, a cable, or a spreader. A spreader is a long I-beam that has a large, heavy ring or loop in the top center and another loop at each end on the opposite side of the beam. The big hook is placed in the center loop; cables hang from the end loops and there is a clevice at the ends of the cables. These clevices fit under the side sill of a car or locomotive so that the lifting force is applied to the center of the car from the bottom on either side in order to balance, or stabilize the weight. A second derrick (usually two are used) or a big D-9 dozer is used at the opposite end of the car being lifted to raise that end with a sling looped under the car coupler, which is located at the bottom center of the car.

Wrecking is generally a slow process because of the tremendous weights of the loaded cars or locomotives involved. Blocks and slings must be carefully and securely set or fastened so there is no slip or loss of control of the load being hoisted. Men who are working in close move back to a safe distance and keep alert, as a broken chain, hook or sling will send the massive weight crashing to the ground, and the lifting boom, suddenly freed from its load, swings wildly and could possibly overturn the machine or the falling car.

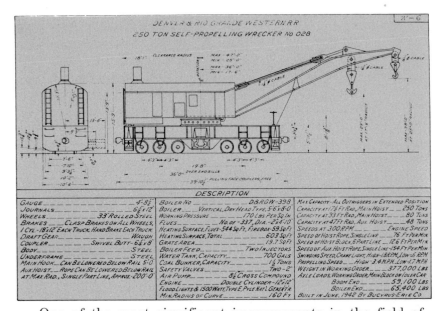

DENVER & RIO GRANDE WESTERN R R
250 TON SELF-PROPELLING WRECKER No. 028

DESCRIPTION

GAUGE _____ 4-8½	BOILER NO _____ D&RGW-398	MAX CAPACITY-ALL OUTRIGGERS IN EXTENDED POSITION
JOURNALS _____ 6½x12	BOILER _____ VERTICAL, DRY HEAD TYPE, 5-6 x 8-0	CAPACITY AT 17½ FT RAD.,MAIN HOIST __ 250 TONS
WHEELS _____ 33 ROLLED STEEL	WORKING PRESSURE _____ 170 LBS PER SQ IN	CAPACITY AT 33 FT RAD, MAIN HOIST ___ 80 TONS
BRAKES _____ CLASP BRAKES ON ALL WHEELS,	FLUES _____ No. OF -337, DIA.-2¼-10	CAPACITY AT 47 FT RAD, AUX HOIST ____ 48 TONS
1 CYL-18x12 EACH TRUCK, HAND BRAKE EACH TRUCK.	HEATING SURFACE,FLUES-544 SqFt, FIREBOX-59 SqFt	SPEEDS AT 300 RPM _____ ENGINE SPEED
DRAFT GEAR _____ WAUGH	HEATING SURFACE, TOTAL _____ 603 SqFt	SPEED OF HOIST ROPE, SINGLE LINE ___ 76 FT PER MIN
COUPLER _____ SWIVEL BUTT-6½x8	GRATE AREA _____ 19.7 SqFt	SPEED OF HOIST BLOCK, 6 PART LINE __ 12.6 FT PER MIN
BODY _____ STEEL	BOILER FEED _____ TWO INJECTORS	SPEED OF AUX HOIST ROPE, SINGLE LINE-154 FT PER MIN
UNDERFRAME _____ STEEL	WATER TANK, CAPACITY _____ 700 GALS	PROPELLING SPEED __ HIGH-3.4 M.P.H. LOW-1.7 MPH
MAIN HOOK__CAN BE LOWERED BELOW RAIL 5-0	COAL BUNKER, CAPACITY _____ 1½ TONS	WEIGHT IN WORKING ORDER _____ 377,000 LBS
AUX HOIST__ROPE CAN BE LOWERED BELOW RAIL	SAFETY VALVES _____ TWO-2"	AXLE LOADS, WORKING ORDER, MAIN BLOCK ON IDLER CAR
AT MAX RAD., SINGLE PART LINE, APPROX-200-0	AIR PUMP _____ 8½ CROSS COMPOUND	BOOM END _____ 59,100 LBS
	ENGINE _____ DOUBLE CYLINDER-12x12	BOILER END _____ 65,400 LBS
	FLOOD LIGHTS & 1500 WATT,TYPE E, PYLE NAT'L GEN'R'R	
	MIN. RADIUS OF CURVE _____ 160 FT	BUILT IN JUNE, 1942 BY BUCYRUS-ERIE CO.

One of the most significant improvements in the field of rerailing railroad equipment was the development of the S-B (side boom) bulldozer. D-9 cats are equipped at one end with a conventional blade, at the other end with a Hyster (cable winch) and on one side, mounted over the track is a collapsible boom. Hydraulic pressure operates the boom which has a lifting line and hook similar to those used on the Big Hook. These monsters are versatile; they can doze a grade, push or roll cars, move rail panels, pull anything and now they can lift as well. Specially built flatcars equipped with a loading ramp, tools, fuel, spare cables and parts are provided to haul these new machines. They are strategically located at intermediate points on the line, and trained operators are provided to operate them. The greatest advantage of the machine, when placed in a wrecking train, is it can make track speed. The old rail bound steam or diesel powered hooks were restricted to 35 m.p.h. with the boom trailing. If you had to run in reverse, or with the boom forward, 25 m.p.h. was all they were allowed. The Side-Boom Cat, loaded on its car can put down its own ramp, walk off, reload the ramp on the car and be ready to go to work in ten or fifteen minutes. After the work is finished it can reach up, get its ramp, walk on the car, pick up the ramp and be ready to roll in the same length of time.

The ordinary derrick train was comprised of six or seven cars, depending on how many cars of rail panels were carried. The derrick was always trained right behind the locomotive, and the boom car followed the Big Hook. It contained the slings, cables, blocks and frogs. Next came the tool car where the smaller stuff was stored; such as torches and gas, pumps, saws, generators, etc. Behind that was the kitchen, diner, sleeper car all-in-one which provided hot meals and sleeping quarters for the car men. Train and engine crews were provided meals as well. A tie car was trained ahead of the rail panel cars. The amount of track torn up determined the number of rail panels required to be used. The prefabricated panels were 39 feet long with rails, joint bars, tie-plates all assembled on the ties, ready to set in place on the grade to restore the track in a shorter time than that required for the section men to do it one piece at a time. A standard caboose was always trained at the rear end of the train for the train crews who were called in wrecking service.

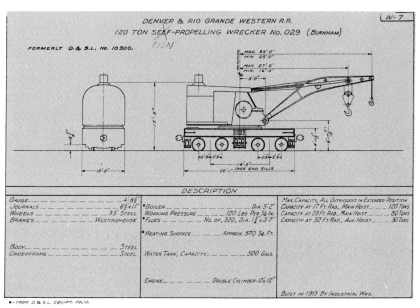

What a monumental mess! This diesel powered, eastbound freight train was running 50 m.p.h. through Green River, Utah, when a heavy load of copper ingots derailed due to an overheated journal (hot box).

The tremendous weight of the train, moving at a high rate of speed, generated an unbelievable amount of momentum. This great force of energy was arrested in a very short time and distance when the wheels of the car left the rails and a general derailment occurred. The amount of destruction was in proportion to the speed of the train, as evidenced by the shattered cars and scattered lading. Thirty-nine cars piled up in this accident.

At the left, "Big Hook" No. 028, lowers its light line at the end of the boom, over a car truck, preparing to rerail a damaged box car. The second, or big hook, on the long boom, is used for lifting heavy cars and locomotives.

The bulldozer at the right side of the track assists at a derailment by grading the track, moving damaged lading, and pushing or pulling the wrecked equipment within reach of the derricks.

The powerful derricks have a great lifting capability, but are limited in their reach. They can only lift a heavy load within a 12 degree radius of the center line of the track.

The use of bulldozers to help clear the right-of-way at a derailment was pioneered by the Rio Grande in 1941. As shown in the above scene, these sturdy crawlers were equipped with winches for pulling and blades for shoving derailed cars within reach of the derricks. Here "Big Hook" No. 028 lowers its boom to make a lift with the light line. Working as a team, these powerful machines made short work of derailed cars and damaged lading. — BOTH JOHN B. NORWOOD

No. 026 is using a cable spreader attached to the hook of the light line and fastened at each side of the west end of the flat deck. No. 028, *Sampson de Grande*, has a cable hitch around the coupler at the east end of the car and suspended from the hook on the light line. A pair of freight car trucks have been placed on the track between the derricks. On a signal from the wrecking boss, the powerful machines will lift the damaged car back on its running gear and have it ready to roll in a "hospital train" toward the repair shop. Both of these derricks were coal fired at the time of this accident. Each was converted to burn oil, and subsequently to diesel powered hoisting equipment.

"Up on the boom and boom'er around right!" shouted the derrick foreman, as the No. 028, using only its light line, easily lifts what is left of a shattered box car. The wreckage will be set aside, to be retrucked later. The splintered lumber at the right will be piled and burned. (BELOW) Two weary trainmen sit on the concrete base of the signal mast at Green River, Utah, waiting for the "Big Hooks" to load a flatcar deck on another car which had just been retrucked. Spike mauls, lining bars, shovels and rail tongs litter the ground around a dual control switch; evidence that the "Gandy Dancers" had been there first. Without the Maintenance of Way forces there to restore the damaged track, no derailment could be cleared.
— BOTH JOHN B. NORWOOD

This photograph shows an example of "short flagging." This trainman is only four rail lengths behind the standing caboose. One hundred and sixty feet is too little distance for safety in non-Automatic Block Signal territory. — DONALD DUKE

6

Rule 99. Flag Protection

A TRAIN OR locomotive stopping on the main track under circumstances in which it might be overtaken by a following train must at once be protected by a flagman (using the required red flag by day and red light by night, and in addition torpedoes and fuses must be used to warn the approaching train or engine). The flagman must immediately go back a sufficient distance to insure full protection. (In the old days this was a judgement decision made by the conductor or the rear brakeman, based on his experience, the weather conditions, terrain, grade, time of day and the expected speed the following train would be running, and at whatever time and place full protection was necessary.) Good rules knowledge and exact compliance was incumbent on the "eagle-eye" whose locomotive wheels exploded the two guns (track torpedoes) and then reacted in time to slow or stop his train in response to the signals given by the flagman ahead.

One bit of old railroad lore told of a formal investigation that was held to develop facts and place responsibility in connection with a "rear ender." The student fireman, who was hep to all the "boomer lingo," testified as follows: "We are comin' down the

A short flag and the failure of an engineer to properly control his speed caused this accident. In this scene, No. 1206 has plowed through the end coach of a Sunnyside Local train at Price, Utah, on December 7, 1916. — S. A. DOUGHERTY COLLECTION

high iron, see, really splitting the wind, when all of a sudden we bust two guns, and we pop around the curve on two stacks of red. The hog jockey put her in the britchin on two pipes to the seashore, gave it the secret works and I joined the birds!"

Just about the same thing happened to "Casey" Jones and Sim Webb at Vaughn, Mississippi, on the old Illinois Central. Short flagging has caused many a pileup, and usually with serious consequences. Several instances come to my mind. Especially the one shown in the old picture entitled "No. 1206 plows through the Sunnyside coach, December 7, 1916 at Price, Utah."

So reads the hand printed inscription on the post card sized photograph of the No. 1206, a Mikado-type 2-8-2 shown standing on the main track at west Price Siding amid the tangled wreckage and splintered remnants of what was a passenger coach trained at the rear end of the Sunnyside Local. Several injuries resulted from that crash. I don't remember if anyone was killed in this rear end collision. The entire scene bears mute evidence of a man's failure to provide flag protection as required by the rules. Or that the hoghead of the eastbound No. 1206 failed to properly control his speed after exploding two torpedoes placed 100 feet apart on the right hand rail in the direction of his movement. Do you suppose he failed to see the red flag being waved frantically in an urgent stop signal? Or did he ignore the "wash out" sign from the flagman? This was non-ABS (non-automatic block signal) single track with a timetable, train order system of operation in effect at the time of the accident. There was no yellow or red block signal warning in advance, as modern signal systems provide today.

There have been many bad, rear end collisions and sideswipes that occurred because the hoghead failed to control his train speed properly after passing a "yellow" or cautionary signal aspect. Numerous accidents have been the result of failure to stop for a "red" or stop indication. Some have resulted from failure to proceed at restricted speed after having passed a stop-and-proceed ABS.

Definition of restricted speed: *Proceed prepared to stop, not exceeding 15 miles per hour.*

Too many enginemen have placed their own interpretation on this requirement and figured they were permitted to make the maximum speed specified under any and all conditions, much to their dismay at not being able to stop short of a broken rail, switch not properly lined, a caboose, box car, or locomotive ahead.

Rule 507: *A train or locomotive stopped by a red ABS must stop before any part of the car or locomotive has passed the signal.* (Not one inch beyond!)

I recall one case, during the progress of a formal investigation being held for a red block violation, where the engineer was going too fast to stop his 3600-class Mallet short of the stop signal. He got by the red block the length of the boiler, stopping so that the cab window was just east of the westward signal mast. He attempted to defend his position by telling the examining officer that he did not get "clear by" the red block with his entire locomotive, but that only the front end had passed it. To which the examiner asked, "How long is that Mallet 2-8-8-2 from the cab window to the front of its pilot?" The hoghead scratched his head and acknowledged, "About 100 feet." To which answer the "brass" replied, "That would be a hell of a long way into a caboose had there been one standing at that ABS."

We had a sort of reverse "rear-ender" early one morning a long time ago. It happened like this: A westbound freight drag came sailing down the hill from Cliff, around a big curve to the left and found the train order board at Woodside in the stop position. A red semaphore indicated train orders for delivery. As soon as the train dispatcher made up his mind about issuing orders to a train he would tell the operator which direction, how many copies to make and the "lightning slinger" would display the fixed signal (semaphore-type) board at stop as a signal to the approaching train of orders for pickup. The operator would then copy what the dispatch' dictated over the telephone, fold the flimsies and tie them in a string loop. The string fit a Y shaped stick, which in turn was placed in a high bracket of an arm extending from a platform built close to the main line. A sort of "automatic" train order delivery device. Before these were placed in service the operators clipped the orders to a cane (wooden) hoop and stood as close to the track as he dared with his arm held high and hoop extended upward along side of the track as the fireman of the onrushing train held tight to the gangway grab iron with one hand and leaned out as far as he could to catch the hoop with his other hand. If that stiff stick hit your face you received a nice welt . . . many a fireman missed his grab. The use of the "automatics" made things a lot safer and easier, only sometimes the string would break when it hit the fireman's arm, and then you had to stop and go back to get your running orders.

That's what happened at Woodside, the string broke, and the fireman yelled, "Stop 'er, the damn string broke!" And of course the hoghead got mad and had a few unkind words to say. At 50 m.p.h. he set a bunch of air and stopped as soon as he could. It took a half mile. When everything came to a grinding halt, the caboose at the rear end was at the telegraph office and that building was located just west of the east siding switch. Just beyond the hand throw switch stood an ABS signal mast and the aspect displayed stop.

This hogger was a young runner and rather impatient to get going and stay ahead of the following train. No one liked to get "spiked," or runaround. He horsed her over and started backing toward the east, to pick up the orders they'd missed instead of standing there on the main line while the head shack walked back to the office to get them. Or until the "Big Ox" at the rear end carried them to the engine. The hogger did not wait for a backup signal from the crummy; as soon as the air released, back he went.

He did not know that he had a red block behind as he could not see around the curve. The red block indicated a following train in that section of track east of the switch. Neither did he know that his rear brakeman was on the ground and had started walking east to provide flag protection for their standing train. Somewhere along about now the conductor should have pulled the air in emergency to prevent the reverse movement by the red ABS. As I said, this young runner was impatient as hell because when the caboose passed the rear flagman, the speed was too high for him to safely get on board, and he was left standing there, yelling and waving his arms in a wild "wash out" signal to stop!

When the conductor heard the yelling and saw the frantic stop signs, he looked toward the east into the bright beam of the headlight of the No. 1710 Extra West. With no thought of pulling the air from the caboose valve in the cupola to stop his train, he grabbed his handbag and lantern and unloaded along the trackside just as the caboose collided with the standing locomotive and made a big mess of itself all over the front end of the extra west.

The hoghead of the No. 1710 had passed a yellow intermediate ABS west of Cliff and had slowed to medium speed as required. He got a real big surprise when the next thing he saw was a caboose coming east, right at him! So he "plugged 'em" and jumped off, landing on his head. He was pretty badly injured as he never worked much after that happened.

They fired the impatient hogger as well as the mighty confused conductor. The rear trainman lost his handbag in the crash as the caboose stove fell over on impact and burned up the wreckage of the "reverse rear ender."

In the old days before ABS (Automatic Block Signals) were put in use on the nations railroads the rear trainman had a vital function to perform. It was his sacred duty to jump off and run back up the track if his train should stop for any reason. The purpose of this mad dash was to warn any following train movement there was a standing train ahead and that they should reduce speed and be prepared to stop short of a rear end collision.

The flagman carried torpedoes (warning devices) which were affixed to the top of the rail and would explode with a loud "bang" when compressed by the wheel of a car or locomotive. He also carried a red flag by day and a red light at night, as well as red fusees (flares). The fusees were used to give stop signals and to ignite and leave burning along the track to warn an approaching train a stop was required. After stopping, the train is required to wait until the fusee has burned out in order to give the flagman time to return to his own train after having been recalled.

Many times a flagman was slow to perform these duties, or failed to go back a sufficient distance to insure full protection and serious accidents occurred.

Now flagging could be a lonely job. Being out there by oneself, especially at night was kind of spooky; like out on the desert or in the dark piney woods, with wild beasts around.

Between Cedar Siding and Verde is a desolate stretch of dry, desert country. Remote and windswept it produces greasewood and chico brush, cactus and a few scraggly cottonwood trees that grow in the bottom of an arroyo, watered only during flash floods.

Sandhouse talk has it that one afternoon a freight drag west stopped at Verde to set out a hot box; the rear shack loped off and ran back about a mile to put down some guns for No. 5, the afternoon flyer.

After setting out the bad order car on the spur, the "eagle-eye" blew the required five long blasts of his whistle to call the flagman from the east, and, as he could not see the crummy at the rear of his train, he waited ten minutes and took off for Mounds to get in the clear for the varnish. The "Big Ox" (conductor) caught the cab on the fly only to find that his rear man was not on board. So on they went, figuring that the missing flagman could hitch a ride on No. 5.

Only what they did not know was that when the flagman heard the recall whistle signal and had started back to his train, he was intercepted by two hungry coyotes who got between him and the safety of his caboose. The terrified man ran for the nearest cottonwood tree and climbed to safety in its branches. The wild beasts took up their vigil beneath the tree. No. 5 came and went and there sat the fearful flagman.

Finally one of the animals left the scene and the poor man took hope that the other beast would give up the idea of having a trainman for lunch and leave as well. Night fell.

The besieged flagman's hopes were dashed at daybreak when he looked down from his perch to see his tormentor still in residence. Soon he was overcome by an even greater fear when he saw the other coyote returning, accompanied by a beaver!

Talk about a near-miss. This incident happened to me once while handling an eastbound drag freight out of Helper. Again, Woodside was the siding involved. We left town around midnight on a Mallet pulling 90 foreign line cars. I had along a "student" (inexperienced) fireman and a gabby head brakeman. At Cedar the Train Dispatcher lined our train into the siding to permit an eastbound "main" train to pass. I was as nervous as hell, not having had much experience at the time and working with green hands didn't do anything to calm me down. I guess I must have been pretty slow getting in and out of the sidings, trying to keep from breaking the knuckles and couplers on what was a big train in that day and age. After the "main" had passed, the dispatch' cleared us out of the siding and we were on our way. We proceeded to the block west of Woodside; it was displaying a yellow aspect. I

A track torpedo is a charge of dynamite wrapped in red paper. The pliable lead straps fasten the warning device over the top of the rail. Called "guns," they explode with a loud bang when compressed by the wheels of a locomotive or railroad car. — DONALD DUKE COLLECTION

slowed to medium speed as required and headed in on a red over yellow. There was no sign or any information that anyone was ahead, so we figured that we were going in to clear for No. 5, the *Exposition Flyer.*

Woodside held about 120 cars and I moved rather slowly as I was not sure of my landmarks or how far I had to go to reach the east block in the siding. There is a left-hand curve in the track, and with all that boiler out ahead of me, my view was limited. I figured I was getting close to the stopping point, so I looked over to the left side of the cab and found my fireman and the head brakeman having a visit. "How far to the block?" I asked. The fireman answered, "I can't see it. There's a train ahead." Well, Jesus, I was right on top of the "main" train that had passed us at Cedar! The dispatcher stuck him in at Woodside to meet No. 5, too!

When he said "train ahead" I grabbed the automatic brake valve, and thank God, I was moving slow enough to stop about ten feet behind the rear coach. It was not required to protect his rear end while standing in a siding, however, the passenger train's rear brakeman had lighted a fusee and was giving a stop signal to those inattentive crew members on the left side of my engine. I was not able to see his signal due to the track curvature and the length of the locomotive boiler ahead of me. Just as I got stopped No. 5 came roaring through the cut making 60 miles per hour!

It does not take much imagination to picture what could have happened had I plowed into the stationary equipment and jackknifed it out foul of the main track, out into the face of the speeding westbound Flyer. Nor does it take much to imagine what I had to say to those careless bastards on the left side. A lot of accidents, loss of life and destruction of property are the result of too much "bullshit" in the locomotive cab. Here is one place where a little inattention can cause a great deal of regret.

Rio Grande passenger train No. 2, the *Scenic Limited*, running by way of the Royal Gorge Route, rolls along at a fast clip east of Dotsero working toward Minturn. During the 1940's the standard consist of the train was a 4-8-4 type locomotive and about 12 cars. — GERALD M. BEST

An eastbound Rio Grande hotshot freight, with five diesel units on the head-end, nears Tunnel No. 18 below Crescent Siding on August 29, 1977.
— RON C. HILL

7

Some Unusual Accidents

THE RIO Grande made a training film entitled *The Trouble at Troublesome* that is a classic example of how absent-minded conversation between two crew members in the cab, aboard a fast moving train, can result in a catastrophy. The film was widely shown as an object lesson for new employees as well as "old heads."

The film was really well made. It was produced by the Publicity Department, using the actual wrecked equipment and the clean up operations filmed at the scene. A crew made up of supervisors was used to portray the employees involved. Some startling special effects made for a realistic crash sequence.

The *SPD*, an eastward second class freight train left Bond on an early morning in May 1953, and proceeded up the river through the rocky, rugged Gore Canyon. Around Azure the sun shone brightly on the peaks of jagged granite in some of the most beautiful country in Colorado. Here, vertical walls of lichen-covered rock ascend hundreds of feet above the wildly rushing torrent.

By the time the *SPD* passed Kremmling at milepost 103 the sun shone right in the faces of the crew in the cab of the big F-7

Four units of an F-7 diesel-electric locomotive are battered and still, half buried in the soft earth along the right-of-way, at Troublesome Siding, Colorado. — JOHN B. NORWOOD

locomotive. The train dispatcher, from his office in Sulphur, lined the east switch at Troublesome and positioned the signals to set up a meet between the *MX (Moffat Extra)* west and the eastbound hotshot. With the control levers on the dispatcher's console positioned to accomplish the meet, the *MX* would have a "red-over-yellow" Automatic Block Signal aspect at the east switch of Troublesome Siding. The speeding *SPD* would receive a "yellow-over-red" or "high yellow" at the west switch to govern its movement eastward to a "red" aspect on the ABS located just west of the east switch.

According to what is known, the *MX* proceeded to head in at the east end of the siding as required by signal indications and timetable and operating rules. The train was about 30 cars into the pass on what looked like a nonstop meet between the two trains, when it became apparent to the head end crew of the *MX* that the *SPD* was still moving at a high rate of speed after passing the caution signal at the west end of the siding. As the story goes, the fireman on the westward train grabbed a red fusee, lit it, and began to wave a frantic "wash out" to the opposing train. As the engines passed one another he reportedly threw the burning flare at the front cab window of the locomotive on the *SPD*. The fireman knew that his train was still fouling the main track at the east siding switch, and knowing the remaining distance to that point, he realized the speeding train could not stop short of a side collision!

And collide they did! With a grinding, rending roar the giant EMD units smashed into the side of a car in the *MX* consist at 50 miles per hour! When the dust had settled and the parts stopped flying, four diesel units were lying on their right sides about 30 feet from the track, battered and still, half buried in the soft earth along the right-of-way. Two separate derailments occurred; one at the east switch and the other about midway of the siding, where equipment of the eastbound train derailed due to slack action, and the derailed cars collided with the *MX* on the adjacent track. Over a million dollars in damage to lading and equipment was the result. There were no serious injuries. It required more than 24 hours to clear the wreckage so traffic could be restored. It took a week to pick up the junk.

At a formal investigation held to determine responsibility for the accident there was testimony by members of the crew that, as the *SPD* left Gore Canyon at milepost 106, the fireman had vacated the front, operating cab. He had walked back through the units to make an inspection before reaching the fast track. This was reasonable in light of the fact that it is difficult to walk in the swaying, pitching aisle of a diesel engine room at high speed. He remained in the trailing cab of the fourth unit. As the train approached west Troublesome at 50 m.p.h., the engineer and head brakeman were riding in the operating cab at the front end. The train was on tangent track for one and one-half miles west of the "high yellow" ABS that required medium speed (a speed not exceeding 30 m.p.h., prepared to stop at the next signal). There was plenty of time to see the caution block and sufficient distance to enable the hoghead to set the air brakes and reduce his train speed and be prepared to stop if the *MX* was still not in the clear of the east siding switch.

The engineer and head brakeman testified that they were engaged in a conversation . . . about how lucky to be called for such a fast, light tonnage train. And all the while their luck was running out! No one saw the "reduce speed" aspect of the west

Derailed freight cars litter the mainline at Troublesome Siding as a result of the speeding SPD sideswiping the MX. — JOHN B. NORWOOD

Looking east at the wreckage of the SPD at Troublesome Siding, milepost No. 101, on the Moffat Route. Note the pillars of a highway overhead bridge ahead of the overturned locomotive. — JOHN B. NORWOOD

An overall view of the derailed equipment at Troublesome. It took a week to pick up and haul away the carnage. — JOHN B. NORWOOD

block, and evidently failed to see the burning red fusee being waved by the greatly alarmed fireman on the westbound extra!

The crew members of the *SPD* were old heads and had worked together over this district for many years. They were familiar with rule and signal requirements. There was no failure of brakes, track or equipment. What caused the sideswipe? Was it really the result of being so engrossed in conversation that both men missed seeing the important ABS aspect? Or were they asleep? Around the "sandhouse" it was rumored the hoghead had been playing poker all night and had lacked adequate rest. A rumor which was not developed in the hearing. In cases like this, no one is going to come "flat-out" and admit he was asleep. One thing I soon learned is that it is damn difficult to stay awake in the nice, warm cab of a diesel locomotive, with their smooth ride and the constant, droning hum of the motors. Crew members have to really concentrate on staying alert, and give their undivided attention to signals and rules.

One of the worst rear enders I was ever involved with happened in the predawn hours of Memorial Day 1952 at Dry Creek, located just west of milepost 119 at Pueblo Yard. It was bad because it resulted in two fatalities and nearly a million dollars in damage to cars, track and locomotives.

The ringing telephone brought me from a deep sleep and my "hello" was answered by the little lady operator saying, "Mr.

Dougherty, there is a derailment at Dry Creek." . . . Very matter of fact, no excitement or any indication of the extent or severity of the accident. With only that much information you'd think some dope ran through a switch and then backed up. A pair of wheels, or maybe all of the wheels of a car derailed. Nothing to get excited over. Like hell! I rode to the site with the Trainmaster and Terminal Supervisor. We had learned that 2nd No. 44 had hit the caboose of 1st No. 44 entering Pueblo Yard. That was as much as we knew when we left the old depot. Certainly we were not prepared for the shocking sight of four F-7 units over on their sides amid the tangled, twisted wreckage of about 50 cars! Or the search for the conductor and the rear trainman of the leading section of No. 44. We found the two bodies at daybreak, crushed beneath overturned cars. It looked like both men had gotten off the caboose and had tried to run away from the track when they saw the blinding headlight of 2nd No. 44 bearing down on them at high speed.

The result of a rear-ender collision at Pueblo Yard on May 30, 1952. In this accident, second No. 44 hit the caboose of first No. 44 at the beginning of the yard tracks. — JOHN B. NORWOOD

Where could they run for safety? On the right were the yard storage tracks filled with "reefers" in dead storage. To the left was the westbound main line and beyond that a deep barrow ditch and a barbed wire fence.

The engineer and head end brakeman of 2nd No. 44 were battered and bruised, though not seriously injured in the collision. The fireman, again in the rear cab! He was not hurt. Both main tracks, the long siding and the Dry Creek storage tracks were torn up for a hundred yards. Many of the cars in storage were damaged by the jackknifing action of equipment in each of the eastward trains, in all, around 50 cars were involved. Ironically, the all-steel caboose of 1st No. 44 bore the full brunt of the smashing impact, lost all of its window glass, but remained intact.

As Road Foreman of Equipment it was my duty upon arrival to see that the injured were taken care of first and then make whatever investigation was possible to determine the cause and results. I had the Car Foreman use my key to open the speed recorder box, remove and sign the tape, after which I signed it and identified the document as to the time, date, location, unit number and the engineer's name. Permit no slip ups here—this was a damn serious business, what with dead and injured employees, thousands of dollars damage and obvious rules violations. All of your evidence had better be perfect. The Interstate Commerce Commission would be involved, as well as the Colorado Public Utilities Commission. When I looked at the speed line of the tape it indicated 42 miles per hour at point of impact, then a vertical line to zero as the unit overturned.

This was a double-track piece of railroad, with timetable, train order operation and an Automatic Block System in use.

First No. 44, an eastbound second class train left Salida carrying the "green," an indication that a following section was running on No. 44's schedule, with the same right and precedence as the first section. Both trains ran over the subdivision at normal speed without incident, the second section right on the block of the leading train. At Pueblo Yard there was a Yard Limit rule in effect.

The first section arrived at Dry Creek and slowed to enter the turnout. The head brakeman ran ahead to line the necessary switches for their route into the designated yard track as the great

Freight cars were spread all over the place following the rear-ender on a very memorable Memorial Day in 1952. — JOHN B. NORWOOD

snake of cars moved along slowly, drifting on a slight downgrade to its final destination. Just before the caboose had come into the clear of the Roger Lead, and while the train was moving three or four miles per hour, the rear end was struck by the speeding second section!

With the type of signal system in use, a train occupying a section of track, or "block" actuates the ABS located at the entrance of that route or block to indicate that the track ahead is occupied. Red block. Stop. If it is a "positive" signal designated by a reflectorized letter "P," permission from the train dispatcher is required before a train or locomotive can enter the occupied track at restricted speed. Signal masts bearing only a number plate may be passed after stopping in the rear of the signal and then proceeding at restricted speed until the next ABS is reached.

Now analyze all of the available information. 2nd No. 44 crew had to know the first section was ahead of them. They were entering yard limits that required reduced speed, moving prepared to stop unless the track was seen or known to be clear and signals indicated proceed.

118

Subsequent tests made by the company signal department experts and by I.C.C. Signal Inspectors of all of the signals involved, indicated that the system functioned properly and found no defects. The company assembled a test train of the identical number of cars, loads, empties and tons pulled by the same number and type of diesel units as 2nd No. 44. The test was made to determine the power and braking requirements necessary to duplicate exactly the speed tape taken from the locomotive of the ill-fated train.

The reader has been made familiar with the operation as to speed and block requirements, yard limits, and the final terminal for the crew. How could anyone, much less an old head engineer, run by a red block at 42 m.p.h., knowing a train was ahead of his train and that it was going to reduce speed in order to pull into a yard track? Or why? He must have known he was facing sure and sudden disaster, if not death.

Again, who will admit to going to sleep? And after such devastating results! In this case there was talk around the sandhouse of a few games of pool instead of the crew getting their proper rest. It was never more true than for hogheads, "the rest of your nights might well determine the rest of your days."

Big Hook No. 024 goes to work on the mess at Dry Creek (Pueblo Yard). Four units of a badly battered F-7 rest amid the tangled wreckage. — JOHN B. NORWOOD

The quiet serenity of Brown Canyon is filled with the growl of 4,500 horsepower motors as three A-B-A units roll a long freight toward Salida en route to Pueblo. These F7 freight units were delivered to the Rio Grande in 1949 by the Electro-Motive Division of General Motors. — DONALD DUKE

The overnight Salt Lake City-Denver sleeper train No. 8, *The Prospector*, drifts down the two percent grade at the base of the Rocky Mountains at Leyden, Colorado, in 1947. — DONALD DUKE

Wearing the original black and gold livery, F-3 class locomotive No. 548, is ready for a run east at Salida, Colorado. — DONALD DUKE

Single expansion articulated No. 3709 works a coal train one-mile west of Castle Gate, Utah. Another articulated is helping at the rear of the train. In 1936, the author worked as a loader at the old Castle Gate Mine No. 3 whose loads may be seen on the siding at the right. — AL ROSE

8

Diesels Replace Steam

ASERIES OF subtle changes began to take place in the types of derailments that occurred, as well as the reasons for their occurrence. Heretofore, I have written about cases involving boiler explosions, washouts, rock slides, head-on collisions, runaways, sideswipes and rear-end smashes, or excessive speed turnovers. In the main, these incidents happened due to natural causes, so called "Acts of God," and failures of man. In nearly every case history there were serious consequences . . . death, injury, and the destruction of track and equipment. Most of the accounts enumerated involved steam locomotives. Diesels were now just coming into common use.

The first regular assigned "F-T" (freight trial) diesel locomotive went west out of Grand Junction in February 1943. Of that I am sure. I was called as fireman on that trip with engineer C.W. (Chick) Pickering at the throttle. Ross Krebs was riding along as Road Foreman.

My experience spans the best and the worst of the world of steam and diesel. I saw the death of the great beasts of fire, smoke and steam and then the advent of the "stink buggy." The old steamers are gone now . . . no more of their sharp, staccato

Lots of black smoke and a rain of hot cinders announce the arrival of Mallet-type No. 3602 battling her way up the three percent grade east of Mitchell, Colorado. This spectacular scene on Tennessee Pass was photographed, in 1940, by award winning railroad photographer Richard Kindig.

Another photograph, also at Mitchell, Colorado, in 1937, is of Mountain type No. 1711 in the swing helper position, while the No. 1510 brings up the rear of a freight. — R. H. KINDIG

The *Scenic Limited*, ready to depart Minturn, Colorado, on July 16, 1938.
No. 3608 will assist road engine No. 1800 up Tennessee Pass. The helper
will be cut off at the summit, and No. 1800 will run all the way through to
Denver. — R. H. KINDIG

exhaust barking their way through the rocky canyons . . . no
more proud plumes of smoke blasting and blackening the eternal
blue sky, or shining silver-white under a frosty moon. Even the
cinders, burned out and lifeless in the barrow ditches, are washed
away by the desert rains. The sights, the smells and the great
sounds are gone and only memories remain. In my reverie I see
the headlight peering like a Cyclops through the pines along the
canyon and among the cottonwoods that grow by the river. I can
still hear that far, far whistle in the silence of the night.

If you never fired or ran a steam engine, or even rode on one,
you will never know the thrill of being a part of those sounds,
scents, and motion. I can still feel the wind whipping around me,
and the sensation of those mighty drivers pounding, reeling off
the miles.

What a sad, mournful thing to see them go, those great, black
and silver monsters, fire breathing dragons, with personalities
all their own. Steam locomotives were responsive to your touch
and feel, one developed a kinship and an affection for them . . .
they are gone now, and they will never return. To hell with
progress!

Four-unit diesel locomotive No. 548 drifts down the two percent grade west of Arvada, Colorado. This photograph was taken in 1945, when the Moffat Route still belonged to the Denver & Salt Lake Railroad and the D&RGW had trackage rights. — OTTO PERRY

A General Motors Electro-Motive Division test locomotive, with crew cars and a dynamometer car trailing, handles 48 cars of freight between Pueblo and Denver on April 27, 1940. — R. H. KINDIG

D&RGW FT (Freight Type) diesel locomotive No. 542 pulls 50 cars of freight across the Coal Creek bridge in 1943. Note the Denver & Salt Lake Railroad logo on the span. The two rail lines were consolidated in 1947. — GERALD M. BEST COLLECTION

Anyone who ever worked steam can tell you those engines had a sense of life and each one differed in personality. With certain locomotives the engineer and fireman got the feeling the locomotive would work willingly and hard in response to their urgings. With others, the crew felt the engines were looking back over their shoulder like a balky horse, as if to question who in hell had the temerity to ask them for an honest effort!

Steam engines had a warmth and smell, coal smoke and hot oil had an odor that clung to your clothes and reminded you that you were a railroad man and it smelled like perfume.

One of the most poignant memories I have of my dad is how his work clothes smelled. Prince Albert in a cob pipe and hot valve oil mixed with coal smoke! I can still relish that delicious aroma. Yeh, I know that the diesel pulls more tons more efficiently, cheaper to operate, that's true. But your clothes stink of diesel fumes and they don't offer the challenge of steam power. There never was the same feeling of pride to walking off the job at the end of a run after parking that multi-unit consist on the tie-up track, like it was to leave that old girl at the water spout, her air pumps panting, and scenting the air with soft coal smoke, a hiss of steam from her open cylinder cocks. That wasn't pollution, that was nostalgia. I couldn't even spell pollution until we started using liquid fuel.

Now let's get back on the subject of how wrecks, or derailments as we are now taught to call them, were influenced or changed by the coming of the diesel engine. (I should use the term "locomotive" because the "engine" has now come to be referred to as the power source and locomotive means the whole works—wheels, chassis, motors, accessories and control cab—the whole unit.)

The railroad industry, as a whole, has for years been neglected as a primary means of transportation. The mass media generally classifies a railroad as old fashioned and regards it as a second or third class means of transport compared to trucks, buses, airlines and waterways. All of these super modes have enjoyed subsidies from the government in one form or another. Well, who built and paid for the super highways? Who dug the canals? Who built the airports? Sure as hell not the truck drivers or owners, and not the airlines. They don't own any airports. While our tax dollars are being spent to build Interstate highways and International airports, the railroads are building, repairing, and financing their own progress out of revenues badly eroded by their freeloading competition. So when the diesel locomotive came along and offered a power source that was much cheaper to operate than steam, American railroads embraced it with renewed hope.

Diesel locomotives could pull longer, heavier trains. More gross ton miles per train hour . . . that's what washes out red ink and buys new rail and ties, cars and more locomotives. Being shipper oriented the railroads wanted to please the customer by building new cars of various types—longer, higher, more capacity—all to attract and hold the business. And in management's exuberance and enthusiasm they engineered in a whole host of unique problems of track-train dynamics. So while the diesel locomotive offered many advantages, it also brought a myriad of problems.

In the old days the ordinary box car was 40 or 50 feet in length. Heavy loads went 80 to 90 tons. Horsepower, or tractive effort, afforded by a big Mallet would let you train 3,000 to 3,500 tons across the desert. Modern diesels handle 8,500 or 10,000 tons of freight in a mile long consist. They pull auto racks of 96 feet lengths, coal and grain hopper cars of 130 to 140 ton gross weight at speeds of up to 70 m.p.h. Today the wrecker goes out more often to clear derailments that were caused by rocking cars, "string-lined" curves, too much draft, or too much buff. Some derailments are even caused by high wind! Did you ever see a tri-level auto rack car try to fly? When 40 to 50-mile an hour winds encounter three air-foil surfaces of over 96 feet in length the flanges are simply raised out of the flangeway and the car derails. A rocking car sets up a rhythmic, or harmonic motion when low joints and high centers, or vice versa, begin to pump energy into the car springs and the damn thing climbs the rail. If you put light loads or empties on the head end behind a high horsepower consist and trail over 5,000 tons on curved track, you will get an L over V effect, sufficient to "string-line" a ten degree curve. You just pull a straight line of what was a curved portion of a train moving around the arc of the curve. A reverse of this condition is high buff caused by retarding heavy tonnage on a descending grade through too much dynamic brake force. The extreme pressure of the weight of the train versus high retardation squeezes the cars out of the flangeway. Many times rails are turned over from this

The *Royal Gorge*, Rio Grande train No. 1, glides downgrade at Colorado Springs, on a halcyon summer day in 1949. EMD No. 5531 was built in 1946; it was the locomotive that was pulling the *Mountaineer*, train No. 19 on November 20, 1953, when it was involved in a head-on collision at Dos Siding. It was later rebuilt as a 1,750 h.p. F-9A. — DONALD DUKE

Rio Grande train No. 1, the *Royal Gorge*, follows the big Alco locomotive No. 6001 over the north switch at Colorado Springs, on its trip to Pueblo and points west. These 2,000 horsepower units were built in 1950 and were used in passenger service between Denver and Salt Lake City. The railroad sold the "A" units in 1967. The "B" units were converted into steam generator cars for use on special trains requiring steam heat. The 16 cylinder engines were replaced with water tanks and two oil-fired boilers were installed in each car body. — DONALD DUKE

L/V stress, and special measures of track construction and maintenance had to be adopted. All in all, it took a great deal of study and many changes to overcome some of the problems that came as a result of dieselization of the railroad.

One of the more serious problems was that of train runaways on grades, caused by confusion of the man running the locomotive. In the old days of steam there was no throttle-dynamic brake combined in a single control. You opened the steam throttle to admit steam to the cylinders when you wanted horsepower to turn the drivers and pull tons on a level track or ascending grade. At the top of the hill you shut her off, dropped her down on the quadrant half stroke and things got a lot more quiet when the exhaust stopped blasting from the stack and the fireman put the blower on to keep the smoke out of the hoghead's eyes.

When the diesel came along someone figured out a way to make the traction motors act like generators on a descending grade; by varying the strength of the electrical field around the armature, and through gearing the motors to the wheels, you could slow or retard the rotation of the drivers and thus provide a braking force sufficient to keep train speeds under control on descending grades. A dynamic or traction brake was a real life saver for mountainous railroads and saved wear on brake shoes. Later on the adoption of a pressure maintaining brake valve, to be used in conjunction with the traction brake, was to effect more savings through greater efficiency and time savings on schedules by almost eliminating the use of car retaining valves on heavy grades.

Now this is where a simple control, for use of power and dynamic brakes, was combined into a single lever. This caused some confusion, however, which resulted in high speed derailments on descending grades.

The transition and braking lever was a single handle on the engineer's control stand . . . pushed forward into the power position or pulled back into dynamic brake. The forward and reverse control is also in a single lever located below the transition lever. Pushed forward . . . go ahead. Pulled back . . . reverse. Ok, we are standing and want to go forward . . . push the reverse lever ahead and place the transition forward to power, release the independent brake and then open the engine throttle

This is the type of control panel built into the cabs of early models of Rio Grande's GP-30, GP-35, GP-40 and SD-45 diesel locomotives. The power-dynamic brake selector lever is at the top right. Pushing it forward places it into the power position, while pulling it back places it in the dynamic brake operation. The throttle-dynamic brake rheostat lever is located in the center of the panel. It is the big lever. The slot at the bottom (center) beneath the guard wire has a white plastic handle inserted in the center position of the reverser. The 26-C automatic brake valve, with its handle in the release position, is at the top left. The off-set handle is the S-40 independent brake valve.

This is the type of locomotive control stand adopted for later models of GP and SD class engines. Note the location change in the dynamic brake control lever. The top slot, with the handle in the left position, illustrates the use of a single lever. Earlier models had a two-position selector switch. The throttle lever slot is located in the center of the panel, while the reverser is at the bottom center of the panel. The automatic brake valve is at the left, with the handle in the service position. The independent brake valve handle is directly below the automatic brake. Note the offset in the operating handle to facilitate ease in use.

to the desired notch. We are moving and about to enter a descending grade. Close the throttle to off, leave reverser in forward position and then pull the transition control lever back to dynamic brake position. Right here is where some hoggers got confused.

The variable dynamic brake requires a regulator or rheostat to increase or decrease field strength, so that the same throttle we were using to supply power is used for the dual purpose of increasing dynamic brake strength. To increase the dynamic brake force we open the throttle, the more we advance the lever, the more resistance we create through increased field strength. In order to develop the increased electrical field the diesel engine speed is increased to the fourth throttle notch and the main generator rotates at a higher speed to supply the juice necessary for more resistance in the traction motor fields.

Mark Twain said "Familiarity breeds contempt, and children." It also breeds carelessness. An engineer gets into a bad habit of doing his job by reflex action; subconsciously, if you prefer, and goes through most of his manipulations of the locomotive controls without conscious thought. As a result, sometimes he finds his train speed increasing on a descending grade because, without thinking, he has closed the throttle at the crest of the hill and failed to place the transition control lever in the proper position for braking, and then thoughtlessly opened the throttle to full power. Hearing the revved up engine the engineer believed he was in the braking notch until his speed increased alarmingly and he came to and made some corrections to reduce speed before overturning his train.

I've had it happen to me and caught it before things got out of hand. I've stood beside other engineers and corrected them before they could get into trouble. On other occasions I've gone out with the Big Hook to pick up the junk and open the line for traffic because the hoghead failed to operate his locomotive controls properly and no one in his crew took any action or made any protest of the high speed before it was too late to prevent a disaster.

In the following chapters are some classic examples of what allegedly happened when the hoghead failed to handle things in a safe and proper manner. The results were devastating!

Moffat coal train PSCX No. 702 moves eastbound at milepost 137.5. These five units of the 5396 lead 9,000 tons of coal down the two percent grade. This place is the scene of the Crater wreck which took place December 25, 1968. — RON C. HILL

9

Catastrophe for Christmas

D ECEMBER 1968 was one of the blackest and most disastrous months in my entire career. The very worst experience I ever had. If there is any substance to the old saw about accidents occurring in sets of three, here is some strong argument in favor of that superstition.

It started off with two alleged personal injuries to crew members on the same train at Bond, involving both the head end and rear end trainmen of an eastbound freight train.

I rode into Bond on a westbound hotshot on December 12th around 12:30 P.M. We came sailing down the main track on a high green block and met this eastward train in the siding, and as our engines passed each other I thought to myself that he was moving pretty damn fast to be leaving town. I knew it was necessary for him to pick up his rear end crew members on the caboose, and at the rate of speed he was running, they would never be able to get aboard. About that time I heard the eastward train air brakes go to the "big hole" (emergency) position and the train ground to a halt. When we pulled down to the crew change point and stopped I learned what had happened . . . at least a part of what took place. As I had surmised, the rear end crew was unable to mount the fast

137

moving crummy. The rear trainman made a valiant attempt to get on the moving caboose and was slammed against the side of the platform breaking his right elbow! A west end conductor, who could run like an antelope, was able to catch the rear grab iron and swing on board the caboose. He pulled the air to stop the train by opening the emergency valve in the cupola.

To further complicate matters, the head brakeman claimed that when he got off his locomotive to go back and inspect his train to ascertain the cause of the emergency stop, he supposedly stepped in a hole along the river bank and injured his back. So, here were two "P.I.'s" (personal injuries) at one crack.

I had my lunch and rode out on the next eastbound train, overtaking at Granby, the freight train carrying the two injured men. The unfortunate crew had experienced a broken air brake pipe on a car. Unable to fix it, it was up to me to walk 100-car lengths through the snow to make repairs. This had to be done in order for the train to pull into the clear, on the siding, for westward traffic thus relieving the congestion that resulted because of the broken brake pipe.

When I got home that night I had a fully developed case of the "flu," and spent the next couple days in bed. I heard over the phone what happened at Clay Siding on the 13th of December. This was one big mess I missed on account of my illness.

As I lay flat on my back in bed, I could see that outside it was a raw, wintery kind of day. I was feeling sorry for myself, and felt like I had been ridden hard and then put away wet, when the paper arrived. My wife handed me the *Denver Post;* on the front page was a color photograph of the pileup at Clay. Looking at that mess of mangled machinery and torn up track made me even sicker than I was. Someone else took care of my duties on that one. Upon returning to work a couple of days later I learned what had happened to train No. 81-13. As the story unfolds, a fast westbound freight, around 3,000 tons, was making time on the ascending two percent grade between the switches at Clay Siding when, "wham" an air pipe under a car about 30 deep from the head end takes this inopportune time to rupture. The conductor and the rear man now start to inspect the standing train to find the cause of the emergency stop. Upon finding the trouble, the head end man starts back, carrying a wrench and a new air hose, to about the

27th car ahead of the caboose, but an air hose won't fix it; the pipe is broken at the thread and will have to be replaced. The bad order car must be set out at Plain Siding.

Ordinary operating procedure and rules compliance would require setting hand brakes on that portion of the train east of the bad order car. Then make a cut behind the car with the broken pipe and take it and the head portion of the train to Plain, the next siding west. The cripple would be shoved on the house track behind the derail and tied down with a good hand brake. After this move the crew should tie the head end of the train down on the siding and go back after the rear portion left tied down at Clay. Then couple the engine on and test the joint, pump up the air pressure in the brake system to the required 90 pounds, and make a set and release. After which test, the crew should then let off the binders they had tied on the standing rear portion of the train.

Now if this sounds pretty involved and like a lot of work, it is, but it is the only safe way. It seems that the crew of this train chose to do things their way. The wrong way! Instead of tying the rear end down, they simply closed the angle cock in the train line ahead of the broken brake pipe. Then they bled the air pressure from the emergency brake application out of the brake cylinders of the rear cars, gave the hoghead a "highball" and proceeded to take the entire outfit to Plain to make the set-out.

One of the first rules of mountain railroading is that you *do not* attempt to handle trains or cars on a grade unless the air system is cut in and charged!

The disabled train advanced to Plain and entered the siding, pulled up to the west house track switch. The brakeman then got off to make the cut behind the bad order car. Of course the slack was stretched and he was not able to pull the pin. He signaled the hogger to back up and give some slack. The rear end crew were setting handbrakes on the hind end to hold it on the two percent grade until the set-out could be made and the head end recoupled to the detached portion. It may be that they failed to set sufficient hand brakes to hold the 27 cars at rest, because when the hoghead took the slack, the rear end started moving slowly down grade, picking up momentum; the farther it moved the faster the cars ran. The trainmen who were setting hand brakes unloaded and away sped the consist of new automobiles, army trucks, shaving soap and corn oil. It flew for almost three miles until it reached a 10 degree curve at east Clay. There it left the rails at about 60 miles per hour and ground itself into a great pile of twisted steel and splintered wood. Shortly, thereafter, the wreckage caught fire. Just a little rules violation! Remember, a little rules violation is like a little pregnancy! A total of $667,000 in damages!

So I missed going to a big one, but I need not have felt left out. Just two weeks hence, I was to be involved in one near Crater that was about the worst in all my experiences. Here is what happened: I had ridden No. 17, the *California Zephyr* into Bond on Christmas Day. A real bummer from the start, riding with an unqualified engineer off the extra list because the regularly assigned hogger had laid off to play Santa Claus. "Hell's bells," I wanted to be off, too! Not only was it my birthday, but my daughter and son-in-law were home for the holidays after spending two years in Chile in the Peace Corps. Road Foremen seldom get their "druthers," so there I was, away from home and loved ones, etc., on Christmas. To make matters worse, No. 18, the eastbound leg, was running late.

Bond, our layover point is just a wide spot in the canyon of the Colorado River and offers little in the way of entertainment or diversion. On a good day you can take a walk, play horseshoes or go fishing, but on bad days you can only play rummy or sleep. It was a bad day. So I was in bed when a loud, excited pounding on my door completely ruined an already rotten day. "Sam! Sam, for Christ's sake get up! The *MX* (Moffat Extra, coal train out of Phippsburg) is in the ditch at Crater. It's bad! The crew is trapped in the cab. I'll get the truck and a stretcher." With that he was gone.

It was 6:30 P.M., and snowing lightly when I got out of bed. With all the information I had already received from the other Road Foreman who called me, I visualized the *MX* had hit a slide in Rock Creek Canyon and overturned in the gorge 500 or 600 feet below the rim of Conger Mesa. In the past, we had joked about this possibility and had concluded that the only wrecking necessary would be to buy a lot of brown paint, climb down to the wreck, paint the cars and locomotive, label them "rock," and then climb out and go home because there was almost no way of pulling such a great mass of weight vertically out of the deep chasm.

140

The derailment was not in the creek. It was in a deep cut where the two percent descending grade snakes its way through the "Big S" curve of ten degrees.

We drove like mad for seven miles over an ice-glazed, graveled road from Bond to Crater. The rescue party was comprised of two Road Foremen, a hoghead, conductor and two trainmen. This crew had arrived in Bond at the same time word of the disaster had come over the train radio. They had volunteered to help, willing to do anything they could to free their fellow employees from the overturned locomotive.

We came upon an eerie scene as our truck stopped along the roadway about 100 yards from the main track. The caboose markers were shining bright, eight car lengths west of the cut through the rocky rib of terrain; no locomotive, but its headlight beam shone through the east end of the cut, shining on the snow covered sagebrush. Jesus, what a ghostlike feeling. Here I had been thinking of getting home for some Christmas but now this!

What would we find in the cab of the overturned locomotive? How bad? What had gone wrong?

The snow on the ground was a foot deep and made plowing through the sagebrush covered flat somewhat difficult. Snow was still falling and the temperature was around 30 degrees. At least there was no vicious wind blowing.

As we drew near the overturned locomotive we heard screams and a voice . . . a woman? Hell, we had no women in train or engine service. Men's voices were screaming . . . the woman's voice was calm and reassuring.

At the upset engine we found the hogger lying on the ground beneath the cab window of the lead unit. Someone had covered him with a quilt. I asked him if he was hurt. He said, "Sam, it's my back. I hurt my back. Get those guys out!"

"Who is in the cab?" I wanted to know.

"A nurse, she came to help us get out."

It developed that she was indeed a nurse. A visiting nurse? Yes. Her folks lived on a cattle ranch a couple of miles west of the location of the wreck and her Christmas visit was interrupted when her father heard the train pass the ranch house at an unusual rate of speed and with a different sound than he was accustomed to hearing. From long years of watching trains pass

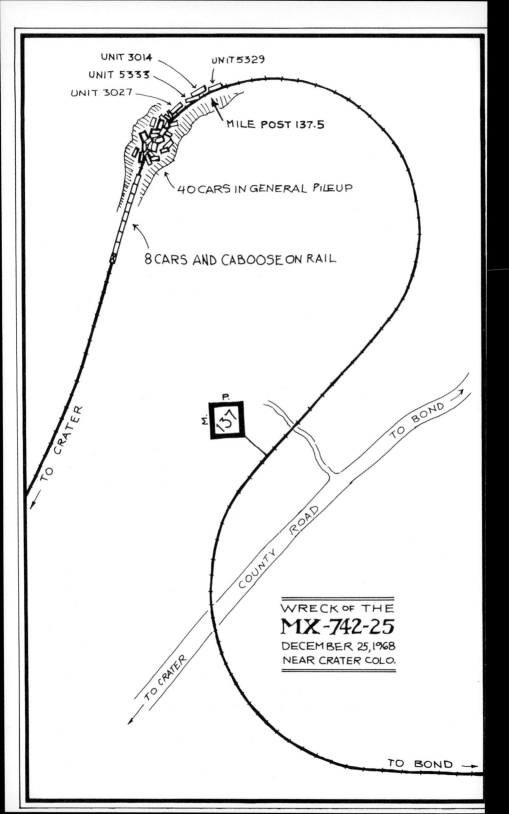

UNIT 3014

UNIT 5329

UNIT 5333

UNIT 3027

MILE POST 137.5

40 CARS IN GENERAL PILEUP

8 CARS AND CABOOSE ON RAIL

TO CRATER

M. P. 137

TO BOND

COUNTY ROAD

TO CRATER

WRECK OF THE
MX-742-25
DECEMBER 25, 1968
NEAR CRATER COLO.

TO BOND →

his home, the old gentleman was alarmed and remarked, "He'll never make it through the 'Big S' at that rate!"

The rancher was right; he didn't make it! When the headlight failed to emerge from the cut the ranch people knew what had happened. The good woman grabbed some quilts and drove to the scene, ready to give first aid and comfort to anyone in need. Her actions were heroic and she no doubt saved the fireman's life by uncovering his face. Using her bare hands, she scooped away the dirt and snow that had filled the cab when the unit overturned and slid for a hundred yards on its left side along the track.

That was a scene to burn into your conscious mind. The dimly lit cab, filled nearly full of rocks, mud, snow and sagebrush. The lady was down on her knees in the muck, working to keep the debris out of the fireman's face with him crying bloody murder. The head brakeman was also on the left side. He was underneath the left cab door which had been torn from its hinges, and the hand railing (a piece of one inch steel pipe), disappearing into the pile of dirt somewhere in the direction of his midsection.

The conductor and rear brakeman had run to the overturned locomotive and broke out a rear window in the cab. By burrowing a little, they were able to get under the unit's left side far enough to scoop the shifting earth from the faces of the two trapped men.

I had previously thought about what I would do in the event such a thing as this ever happened. But this time the nightmare was real. The former daydream was now a reality. You do what you have to do, with first things first. So climb down in the darkened cab and turn on the lights. The doorway opening is packed full of dirt, and will have to be dug out. Break out the windshield glass, but first get some help so we can get the engineer on a stretcher and to the nearest ranch house and out of the cold . . . he has a back injury, so roll him gently on the litter. Next put in a call for a doctor and an ambulance. Get me a sledge to break the heavy glass . . . get some shovels. By now the section men have arrived to help, but with so much rock and earth filling the cab area it was difficult for more than one man to shovel in such a cramped space. The way the units were lying on their side, the dirt kept sifting down and continued to cover the faces of the injured crew men.

Working in relays, sweating and puffing in the high, cold

A catastrophe for Christmas. The Big Hook gets ready to lift the SD-45 No. 5329 back on the iron at milepost 137.5, three miles east of Crater, Colorado. — S. D. SMITH COLLECTION

This was the scene at Crater, Colorado, on December 26, 1968. The No. 5333, in the foreground, slid down the rails and passed the two GP-30's that were ahead of it. — S. D. SMITH COLLECTION

mountain air, the rescue crew uncovered the unhinged cab door and removed it. Now for the hand railing . . . Thank God, it was not stuck in the brakeman's liver, after all. To hear him caterwauling made one believe it had been. The ambulance arrived and two paramedics helped us put the man on a blanket and ease him out through the front window of the cab. He sure looked like hell—muddy and bloody, but fortunately with no serious injury. Now the crew went to work uncovering the fireman.

The seats on the left side of a cab slide horizontally on a track-mounted frame and are attached low on the side panel. The seats had slid together, pinning the fireman's feet between the supports, and it was impossible to budge them. So, more muck had to be shoveled in order to clear the area just enough to place a track jack under the edge of the seat and force the braces apart to free him. He was hurt . . . a broken hip socket. He shook from the cold and then sweat from the pain and begged for help. He hurt like hell and he didn't care who knew it.

Through all of this, the little nurse worked calmly and with great professionalism to give aid and comfort to the injured crew members of the ill-fated *MX*. Her help was of great value and we cannot praise her enough for her contributions.

When the fireman's feet were freed he was carefully placed on a blanket and passed out the front window into the waiting hands of the ambulance crew. In spite of our care he remained in great pain, and we were all relieved when the ambulance started for the hospital.

It took around two and one-half hours of intense effort by all concerned to free the trapped and injured men from their predicament. Now to put all the pieces together and develop a cause of all this damage, grief and pain.

Train No. 742-25 consisted of 48 cars of coal and a caboose. It was being pulled by four units: two GP-30's and two SD-45's. Big stuff . . . new SD's. The first unit was over on its left side, half of the front end buried in a pile of debris she had plowed up and pushed ahead of her nose as she slid along the vertical wall of the cut. The second and third trailing units were still coupled to the head end, lying on their left sides against the side of the cut, and partially covered by coal. The fourth unit had flopped on her right side and slid down the rails, passing the two units that were

The remains of 40-car loads of coal were packed in the deep cut at milepost 137.5, east of Crater, Colorado. — s. d. SMITH COLLECTION

ahead of it. Fuel oil was knee deep. I remember that while digging out the cab, one of the workmen lit a cigarette and I nearly bit his head off yelling "put that God damned thing out!", with enough emphasis to stop his careless habit forever.

Of the original 48 loads, only eight cars remained upright and on the rails. Forty were jammed into a compact mass that filled the deep cut to overflowing . . . coal piled to the moon. The heavy metal car bodies were torn, broken, twisted and smashed beyond recognition! All that destruction heaped in the space of ten car lengths!

As the crew went about the excavation of the men, I had, while being "spelled," given close attention to the cab controls, their position and condition. In the presence of the other Road Foreman, I had removed the paper roll of speed recorder tape from the locked box and had him date and sign it for identification. After the injured men were taken care of we removed the tapes from the other overturned locomotives.

The why? When we got a look at the speed lines on those "tattle-tale" tapes and noted the position of the cab controls of the operating unit we got a pretty good picture of what took place. I was physically ill, partly from hard manual labor, partly from the cold, the snow, the horrible scene of the accident, and partly from grief and frustration. I sat down on a rail and cried.

Get the whole picture. This is a branch line railroad without Automatic Block Signals. This location lay on a two percent descending grade with a 20 mile per hour maximum speed imposed due to the heavy grade and severe track curvature . . . steep and crooked. There are rocky cuts and deep canyons. It is good deer country—covered with pinon and cedar trees, and oak brush and sagebrush flats. There are a few hay fields where ranchers feed their stock. This is Christmas, and red and green lights frame the ranch house porch and windows. It is now snow covered, looking like an old, favorite scene of the season . . . spoiled entirely by this huge, ugly mass of metal piled in grotesque shapes.

A two percent descending grade requires an automatic air brake application and lots of dynamic brake buff force to retard 4,500 tons and hold the speed at its safe level. It is exacting, but easy to do if you know how, know the road, and give it your constant attention.

The speed line on the three tapes we recovered from the wreck all indicated a maximum of *56 m.p.h.*!!! Reducing to 53 m.p.h. at the time the wheels left the rails at the point of a 10 degree curve. Milepost 137.5 was the point of derailment.

The locomotive throttle was in Run 8. Wide open! The reverser was in forward and the transition lever was in power . . . not in dynamic brake position as required. It was no wonder the old rancher was concerned. He recognized the difference in the sound of a locomotive in full power as compared to one operating in dynamic brake.

There is a steel guard wire on the control panel between the throttle lever and the transition-dynamic brake lever. So when the engine overturned to the left, the engineer was thrown forward off his seat and in that direction. His knee or possibly his elbow struck the guard wire hard enough to bend it upward into a position where it blocked the throttle lever slot in the panel, thus preventing the throttle from being closed to idle without bending the guard wire down to its original position. Pretty conclusive evidence of where the throttle was at the time the derailment occurred. That steel wire was 3/8-inch spring steel and not easily bent. The transition lever was in power (Run 1). The automatic brake handle was in emergency, which was later testified to in the formal investigation that ensued. It was also borne out by the speed line on the tape when it indicated a drop from 56 m.p.h. to 53 m.p.h., just before she left the rails.

Those tapes presented a clear picture of miles run and speed of movement. From the top of the hill, eastward for ten miles through Egeria Canyon, the descending grade is only one percent. Here you can hold the speed to the required 20 m.p.h. by using the dynamic brake only. From milepost 150 to 141 the tapes indicated an overspeed violation of from five to seven m.p.h. in excess of the authorized speed. Not too much regard for rules here, is there?

At milepost 141 the grade eases to about .4 of one percent, a short length of "flat," and it is sometimes necessary to go to the "off" position with the dynamic brake, and then go into "power" and open the throttle a couple of notches and pull the trailing tonnage through the "flat." Crater Siding is located at milepost 140; it holds about 60-70 cars . . . still on the "flat." At the east end of the siding the grade increases to two percent. When the trains leave the lighter gradient the engineer should close the throttle, moving the transition lever from "power" to "brake" as the big trains roll on to the heavier downhill portion, and get ready to apply the air brakes on the cars to maintain a speed of 20 m.p.h. through the first curve of the "Big S."

The speed tapes indicated at a point on line where some retardation was necessary, the No. 742-25 was in "power", pulling, and the speed curve started upward on the graph . . . fast! Thirty miles an hour at the west switch at Crater. Forty at the east switch and climbing, going up, 42, 45, 50! This was at the time the train passed the ranch house . . . wide open, down grade!

Why didn't someone in that cab say something? Or take some positive action? Where was the rear end crew when the telegraph poles started going by like a picket fence? From MP 140 to MP 137.5 is two and one-half miles, and at the rate of speed they were traveling it took them three minutes or more. Why was there no protest? These were all experienced, promoted and qualified

148

railroad men, "old heads." Why? Formal testimony, later, gives some clues.

The apparent failure of the other crew members to make a protest or do something to prevent disaster seems to bear out an old theory of mine. They would rather die than open their mouths! How in the world could anyone, conscious, sober and alert, sit quietly by while approaching a ten degree curve at such a terrific rate of speed? Thirty-six miles per hour over maximum permissable speed is disasterous!

The formal investigation into this catastrophe lasted for three days. It shed little light on the true cause, and it is my studied opinion that the whole truth was never told.

It took two Big Hooks, two side boom dozers and three ordinary Caterpillar tractors a full 48 hours to set the units to one side, pull out the broken, twisted mass of metal that had once been coal hoppers, doze the spilled coal out of the cut and relay the track panels to open the line for traffic.

One of the duties of a supervisor, upon reaching the scene of a derailment is to carefully survey the junk, lading, damage to the track and equipment, and get car numbers. Then make some sort of an estimate as to how long it will take to move the stuff, rebuild the track and start running trains again. It costs several hundred dollars for every hour the main line is out of service. Consider first the shippers and their delayed traffic and damage claims. Car per diem and crew requirements . . . held away from home penalty. There are many items to figure into your total cost besides the damage to the track and equipment. Supervisors pride themselves on being able to give the Chief Dispatcher and the other "high brass" a good, close estimate of how long it will take. In the past I had made a lot of close guesses. I goofed badly on this one.

After we had taken care of the injured men, we were then able to devote more time to looking over the mess we faced. In the cold and dark, with snow falling, and I guess pretty much in shock; sick from physical exertion and frustration, a call came from Denver by radio asking for a figure on how long it would take to get the line open. I informed the Chief Transportation Office and the General Manager "Christ, it will take a week!" Thinking, I suppose, that there was no way to get a Big Hook to the west side of the pileup and therefore, only being able to work one on the east end, well, it looked bad. I overheard the GM in the background say, "God made the world in seven days!" I never did live down the stigma of being the Road Foreman who missed his guess by five days! However, it did take a week to retruck and rerail the four units and to pick up and load the scraps of what had been coal cars.

So, I got home on New Years Eve after having left on Christmas Day. I had been sent some clean clothes, packed by my wife and brought along by my boss. After all of the picking up and rebuilding was completed, and traffic had been restored, we put the diesel units and scrap cars in a "hospital" train and dragged it slowly over the division to the repair shops. Guess who got to spend several more hours riding along to see that all went well? The Road Foreman of Equipment.

With two crew members in the hospital it was necessary to start a formal investigation immediately (five days is the maximum time allowed by union contract) and then they recessed the hearing until the injured employees were able to attend and answer inquiry into the why and wherefore of the derailment. In the interim we decided to make some tests, using an exact duplicate of the locomotives, cars and tons of the ill-fated *MX* 742-25.

What we wanted to develop from the tests was how many options did the hoghead have to slow or stop his train before reaching the point of overturning. By using a blown-up reproduction of the tape taken from the recorder of the No. 742-25 as a guide, we brought the test train speed up to 30 miles per hour at the west switch at Crater, and then by using the independent brake, applying 45 pounds cylinder pressure, we were able to reduce the train speed to 12 m.p.h. at the east switch . . . in just over one-half mile. On the second trial run we utilized the dynamic brake and were able to slow the train to ten m.p.h. in the same distance. On test number three, a minimum air brake reduction of six pounds brought the big train to a stop in three-quarters of a mile. The two final tests were made by using an emergency air brake application. The first was initiated from the locomotive brake valve and the second by using the conductor's valve in the caboose. We brought the 4,500 tons to a dead stop within 30 car lengths, about 1,500 feet. The two Federal Inspectors

150

Rio Grande No. 5333 back in the harness, after the wreck at Crater, pulls the NORX No. 755 up the big hill at Mitchell, on the Royal Gorge Line.
— RON C. HILL

who were along were very much impressed. The tests clearly indicated what an engineman could do, if he used the available means to properly control his train speed within safe limits.

At the formal hearing both the engineer and the fireman admitted to spending some time in a local bar and to having a few beers. The other crew members did not admit to the use of intoxicants. Their big problem lay in their failure to call the hogger's attention to the provisions of Operating Rule No. 821-A:

"Employees in a position to do so must call the engineman's attention to any failure to comply with the rules. Should the engineman fail to comply with the rules or become incapacitated, any member of the crew must take appropriate action, stopping the train if necessary."

The bill for this failure came to $770,000. That figure covers the loss in track and equipment only, in addition there was wrecking expense. The cost in pain and lost employment for the employees was much higher. Some Christmas present!

As a result of this disastrous series of derailments, a General Staff meeting was called and the "brass" from each division met and pondered. The overall consensus was the need for better operating rules training, and mandatory compliance to those rules. A new method of written testing on operating rules was devised and placed in use. It was quite a revelation to see some old head enginemen and conductors, who had for years affected a "know-it-all" attitude, now be required to take these tests two or three times before making a passing grade of 85 percent. I guess that the beginning of true knowledge is to find out just how damn little we do know and start from there!

The railroad soon noted a great improvement in performance. Accidents due to man failures took a dramatic drop.

It was obvious from the testimony given that the catastrophe at Crater was the result of a complete disregard for adhering to speed requirements and operating rules governing the conduct of employees while off duty. A "few beers" and a big steak can create an almost comatose condition and give a false sense of security. This, coupled with riding in a nice, warm cab, the droning hum of the engine, plus the fact of little rest before going on duty, is a mind numbing set of circumstances. It is easy to see how a hoghead, confused by a simple locomotive control, could make a serious mistake. It has happened in a couple of other instances at different locations. The derailment at Nolan, on the Utah Division, is a perfect example, and it was a bad one.

In an accident somewhat similar to the one at Crater, 56 cars of an eastbound hotshot freight train piled up at the Nolan Tunnel on a two percent descending grade west of Helper. In that case, no use of intoxicants was involved, and also, the locomotive did not overturn. It broke off and stayed on the rails. There were no injuries and *only* $500,000 damage resulted.

A third case of confused operation happened somewhat later on Minturn Hill just west of the famous Tennessee Pass. In this instance it seems the engineer came out of the tunnel at the top of the hill onto a three percent grade in full power. It looks like he forgot to go to dynamic brake position with his transition lever and opened the throttle wide, thinking I suppose, that he was increasing the dynamic brake resistance. When the speed got up around 35 miles per hour (15 m.p.h. is the maximum here) he plugged the train air brakes (went to emergency) and because some idiot had apparently blocked out the "ER" (engine run) relay the engines did not go to idle speed, as the system was designed. With five units in full power, pulling the heavy train down that kind of a grade, well, the speed increase overcame the holding power of the brakes and away he went! As the metal shoes ground away, clamped tightly against those spinning steel wheels, his braking effort reduced and his speed increased. The conductor cut the caboose off when he noted the air pressure down and the speed up. A deadhead crew, riding on the trailing units of the runaway train, got off at around 40 miles per hour. That is, all except the deadhead hogger. He was old and fat and long past the age of unloading on the fly. So he ambled over from the second unit he had been riding on this wild ride, into the operating cab of the lead unit and found the engineman in apparent shock. He reached over the controller to close the throttle and then jerked the reverser back into reverse position, "plugging the main generator" and thereby sliding all of the drive wheels until she slid to a stop, just short of pitching over Pando Flat onto the three percent. It prevented the train and engine from overturning, but it flattened the wheels to the extent that all had to be built up (by welding) on the spot before the locomotive could even be moved to a repair point.

Other railroads experienced similar "man failures" due to confusion of a simple power control and steps were taken to order locomotives that had separate levers for dynamic brake operation.

Rio Grande hotshot freight (west) coming out of Tunnel No. 29 east of Pinecliffe, Colorado. — RON C. HILL

10

Cadillac Point

THE READER has visited the scenes of some major derailments up to this point. But many other mishaps of a lesser magnitude or minor nature have occurred. Some of these stand out in my memory because they were either unusual, spectacular or downright humorous. Funny, like a broken leg.

One such instance involved a man, nameless of necessity, who got tangled up with a hotshot, westbound freight train early on a cold and snowy morning at Winter Park. As the big EMD diesel locomotive came rushing out the west portal of the Moffat Tunnel at 40 per, the hoghead spotted a pair of automobile headlights shining up at him from between the rails of the main track, just east of the east siding switch. There was no time or space to stop! "Plug 'em" and get out of the seat in case something came flying through the front windshield! Or worse, some of the junk gets jammed into the facing point of the switch and turn the old hog upside down. That has happened. "Ba-Loom!" Anyway, the Caddy went flying down the track, and was all battered to hell. When the train stopped the poor hoghead, badly shaken, got off and started back to see if anyone was killed or injured and if the rails were turned over or wheels derailed . . . a real "gut churning" experience, I can tell you. You hate to find what has happened in that splintering crash; you would just rather not go. But, hell's bells, you must!

Well, the engineer and the head brakeman walked back and were happy to meet the driver and his lady friend passenger alive and unhurt. They got out before the collision, but the car was a total wreck. It had been borrowed from a friend, and so was the woman . . . the wife of another friend! What a spot to be in! How could the hapless motorist explain driving up a snow covered railroad track for a thousand feet beyond the highway crossing at 2:00 A.M. in a borrowed car and with someone else's wife?

One tale leads to another. Speaking of the poor guy's Cadillac, did you ever see a more pitiful sight than eight brand spankin' new cars with their tops caved in . . . totaled out? Well, on one cold day the *LSD* left Denver for points west and the first five or six cars were tri-levels loaded with factory fresh Cads. It was about dark when the four unit EMD came gliding around a left-hand curve in Fraser Canyon and its headlight revealed that a big chunk of real estate, from the right side of the canyon wall, had moved out onto the main line, right into their path! With no time to stop, the hogger did his best. He went to the "big-hole" position and before he could even slow down, "Ker-Blam" he hit the huge pile of granite boulders, derailing all four of his units and five of the trailing cars of Detroit's finest. Nobody was hurt and there was only minor damage to the locomotives. The trailing auto racks were off the rails and upright. Several rail lengths of track were torn up, but the new Cads were still in place on the cars which had tipped slightly to the right, toward the cliff side. It looked fairly easy to rerail the units by simply pulling them toward the west where we could frog them onto the undamaged track. We figured to pull the derailed cars back toward the east so that new track panels could be relayed. Only we had some bad luck!

When we coupled onto the derailed cars we failed to recognize one of the fixed principles involved. If you pull one end of a string that is lying in a curve it will straighten out across the arc. These cars were standing in a curve on the ties of the damaged track, but still conforming to the configuration, and when we gave them a

156

pull toward the east they assumed the tangent position: straight. They tipped over against the unyielding canyon wall . . . bashing in all of those beautiful tops and breaking door glass and windshields. Shards of broken glass can still be found in the crevices of that rocky cliff, now dubbed "Cadillac Point."

There were many colorful names given to points of interest or of natural beauty. Nearly everyone is familiar with the Royal Gorge, the Moffat Tunnel, Glenwood and Ruby Canyons—all famous locations on the Rio Grande. It is the little known places that I would like to mention. Like the "Big Ten", a magnificent 10 degree curve located between Rocky and Clay. It was on this piece of track where two train derailments occurred because of high winds. To prevent more wrecks due to hurricane force gales, a barricade or windscreen was erected. Old, wornout ballast cars were loaded with dirt and spurred out on an especially built track adjacent to the main line. It worked like a charm by damming the wind flow across the Rocky Flat.

It was my idea to pile up an earthen dike around the inside of the curve and then plant grass to hold the soil in place when the strong winds would blow. Our General Manager improved on my original plan by placing earth in these old junkers and then leaving them on a spur track as a permanent windbreak. He ordered the cars painted a neutral buff color to blend with the background. When I suggested planting flower seeds in them to create 21 of the world's largest planter boxes, he vetoed my brainchild and ordered the maintenance of way men to salt the earth with Nalco (weed-flower killer). So I felt the best part of my idea was rejected.

"Sugar Slope" is just east of Tunnel No. Two where an eastbound freight train had an L/V (lateral over vertical or too much dynamic brake buff force) type of derailment that jackknifed a long car-short car combination out of the consist. Thirteen cars stacked up, five went over the bank and eight of them were jammed tight into the rocky bore of the tunnel. A box car load of sugar rolled down 200 feet of steep slope, and the hillside looked like a ski run, white with snow.

Mammouth Creek was renamed "Martini Gulch" after seven tank cars of wine overturned and spilled into the rushing mountain stream near milepost 48. A "pop out" (receiving end of

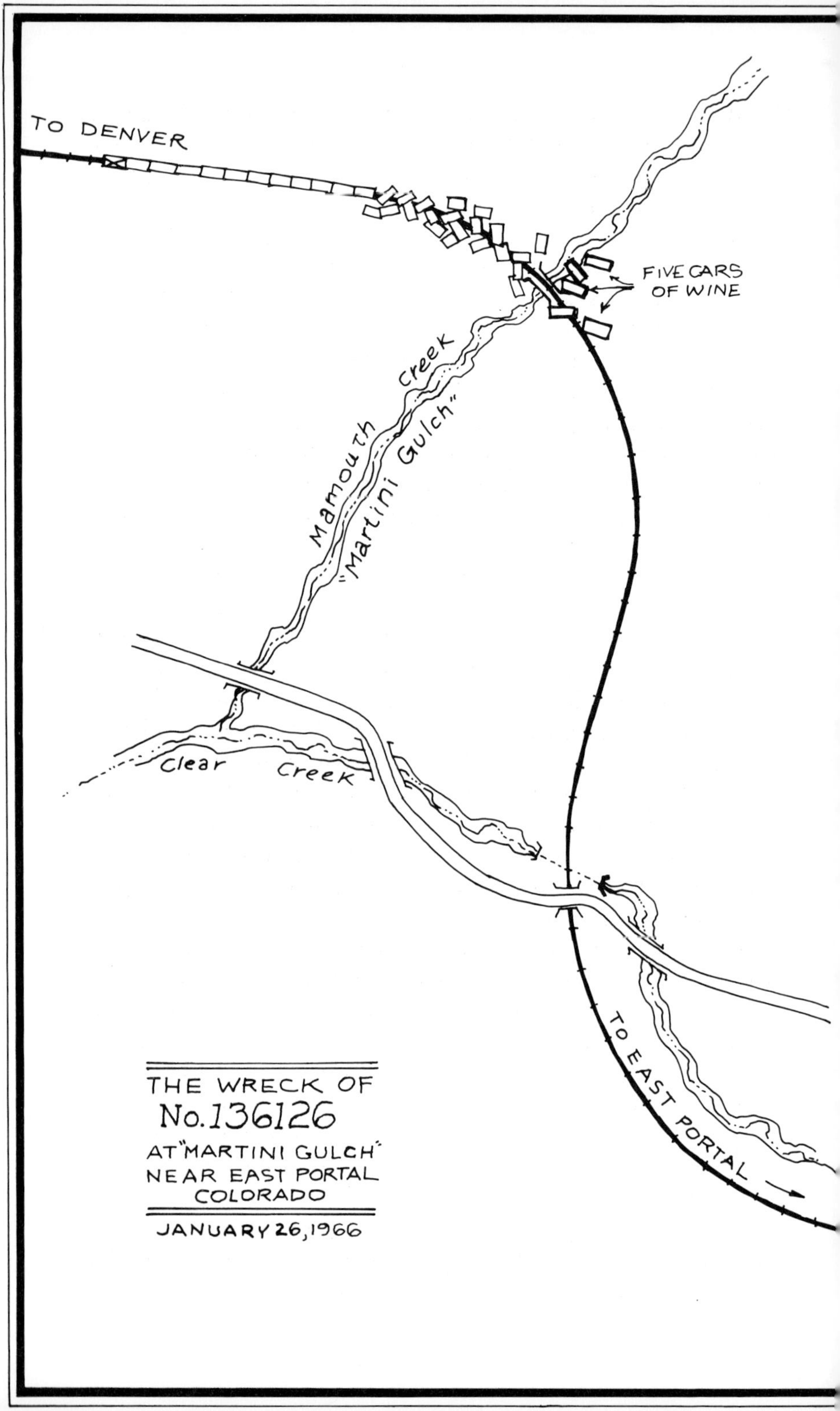

TO DENVER

FIVE CARS
OF WINE

Mamouth Creek
"Martini Gulch"

Clear Creek

TO EAST PORTAL

THE WRECK OF
No. 136126
AT "MARTINI GULCH"
NEAR EAST PORTAL
COLORADO

JANUARY 26, 1966

the rail broke under traffic) had piled up 27 cars. When I came on the scene, I found several local residents had arrived ahead of me. They had been there long enough to partake of many samples of the juice of the vine and were busily engaged in filling some five gallon cream cans with the gushing vintage. To be on the safe side I told them they could not take the stuff; they were stealing.

"Pour it out," I told them.

They argued that it was only going to waste and why not save it. Hell, it may not have been fit to drink, or if they all got drunk and froze to death, they could have come back and sued the company for giving it to them. It is dangerous to be a good samaritan with salvage. Your generosity could backfire.

My dad once told me about a derailment down south that happened a long time ago. It seemed that among the wrecked cars were some loads of "high wine" (champagne, I guess). Anyway, the car knockers, gandy dancers and the train crews got into the stuff and everyone on the scene got so drunk that the rerailing was postponed for three days! Ah, for the good old days!

Another derailment at East Portal, during a blizzard, presented some unusual problems other than working in a minus 30 degree wind chill factor and driving snow. In the pileup, there were three grain hoppers filled with bulk, granulated sugar. It had spilled all over the wreckage and right-of-way, and of course mixed with snow it stuck to everyone's shoes and clothing. The cab of the engine was an inch deep in syrup. The floors of the kitchen and diner were just as bad. Some of the sugar was salvaged (scavenged) by the crews, but most of it was wasted.

East Portal was one hell of a place to have trouble in bad weather; 9,000 feet elevation and in a canyon below James Peak, the snow lies throughout the short summer. The operator at the fan house told of taking his family to Denver once for a three day, Fourth of July celebration and missing the entire summer!

Temperatures, in the months between October and May, get pretty low at that elevation. When driven by a 30 mile an hour wind the snow flakes cut like knives. A man is forced to turn his back and walk in reverse, as the gale just tears the breath out of you and your eyes stream so you can't see anyway. On one occasion, now get this, it was 10:00 A.M. and a trainman was trying to signal a hogger to back three units to a joint with

After six miles of smoke and darkness, Rio Grande No. 3109 emerges from the west portal of the Moffat Tunnel at Winter Park, Colorado. The large headshield on the Automatic Block Signal placed on the wrong side of the main track to improve the view of the signal aspect for westward trains.
— RON C. HILL

A typical snowy day at Winter Park, Colorado, as coal train Moffat Extra 712 East follows the No. 5365 up the heavy grade. — RON C. HILL

another unit. But he was unable to pass a signal using a burning, red fusee, as he was not visible 150 feet away due to the wind blown snow!

Come to think of it, I can't recall ever having a derailment at or near East Portal in the summertime. I guess it was because the season is so short.

In the old days before the use of dynamic brakes and the maintaining brake valve, trainmen had to walk the tops of the cars and place the retainer valve handles in the heavy holding (20 pound) position to permit the engineer to keep the train brakes applied while recharging his brake pipe. At times the fierce wind was so strong a man couldn't even stand on top of a box car! Thus a number of locations were named Windy Point or Windy Gap by the working crews.

Each division had a "Deadman's Cut" or "Deadman's Curve," usually in commemoration of a grisly find or tragedy that marked the spot. "Shaw's Cut", on the old third division, was the location of an early day runaway and pileup of a narrow-gauge freight train whose engineer met his fate there and so lends his name to that place.

Rio Grande narrow-gauge No. 480 works eastbound with a train of empty stock cars and is about to enter the snowshed at the west end of Marshall Pass. —JOHN KRAUSE

11

Marshall Pass Memories

THE NARROW-GAUGE is gone now. No more smoke on the big hill called Marshall Pass. No more rotary plows eating their way through the mountainous drifts. The rusty little rails have long since been pulled up. Just a few rotting timbers mark the location of the old snowshed at the top of the Pass where towering Mount Ouray looks down on the deserted site. Once a telegraph office and a turntable were found inside the shed, lodged in perpetual gloom. At Marshall Pass railroad men struggled against the worst of nature's elements.

Poncha Junction and Mears, Grey's Siding, Shawano Tank and Sargent are names from a memory of blasting stacks, of hissing steam, smoke, fire, and courage. Only cinders and rotting wood remain, along with memories of little engines and big men.

My narrow-gauge experience is limited to the period of time between 1952 and 1956 while working as Trainmaster at Salida. At that time we were hauling limestone out of the Monarch Quarry daily and also handling some coal and lumber out of Gunnison: about one train a month. During the fall, there was some livestock movement.

One day in March of 1954, Harry Egley, Chief Dispatcher at that time, called me in his office and asked me about moving 30 cars of Texas steers from Salida to Gunnison. Inasmuch as we had not operated a train over the Pass for a month or more, and knowing the kind of snow conditions we would encounter on the big hill, I suggested we first run a plow train over the line to knock out the bigger drifts.

The plow train was called for 04:00 with two engine crews, a train crew and some section men for snow service. We put No. 480 on the point as it was equipped with a front end wedge plow. We trained the drag-spreader behind the lead engine and put a caboose behind the spreader for the section men to ride keeping them out of the weather, since they had to operate the spreader wings. Another 480-class, having no wedge plow, was trained next in the consist and the crew caboose was at the rear. We got out on the call and had no trouble reaching Mear's Junction, where we filled both engine cisterns with water before making our assault on the "big hill." The track was clear of snow for a mile west of Grey's Siding. It was there we found the first drift. It was 20 feet high and packed as hard as ice. We rammed into that mountainous pile at 20 miles an hour and ground to a halt in only a few feet. The procedure for plowing was to have two engines coupled so that when you hit a heavy drift and got stuck, the hogger on the No. 2 engine could horse her over and back out, pulling the No. 1 engine free and then take another run at it. Only in this case the plan misfired. When No. 2 reversed his engine and opened his throttle wide, the little wooden caboose we had placed between the locomotives for humanitarian reasons to protect the poor section men, pulled in half! So help me. The draft gear, front trucks, end beam, platform and all pulled out, separated, and the body and rear trucks were still attached to the No. 2 engine, skidded sickeningly down the rails! A total wreck! I never heard the last of that. I was almost fired for wrecking that caboose. It seems someone in the Traffic Department had promised the little crummy to a railfan club and no one could understand why we had it between the locomotives in the first place or how we could do so much damage.

After chaining the wreckage together, we pulled the sorry remains of the caboose back to Grey's Siding with the No. 2

Deep snow on Marshall Pass, Colorado, required two 480-class engines to handle the Jordan Spreader. — ROBERT W. RICHARDSON

Winter scene at the top of the Marshall Pass hill. Rio Grande 480-class pushes a flanger to clear the line. — ROBERT W. RICHARDSON

Inside the snowshed at Marshall Pass. The No. 489 pants patiently in the thin air at 10,856 feet elevation. — JOHN KRAUSE

engine and left it there, sitting battered and useless on the side track.

It was late afternoon when we reached the east end of the snowshed at Marshall Pass. About two feet of snow covered the rails in the entrance, and so there was no way for us to tell that a foot of ice lay under the snow. When our train went charging in and the big plow hit that resistance the little hog reared straight up and turned sidewise to the track, with the drag-spreader derailing behind it.

The crew got down to assay the problems involved in rerailing the equipment, as I went trudging through the shed toward the telegraph office to tell the Chief Dispatcher of our predicament. The closer I got to the office the more I noticed how much daylight there was in that dark tomb. Ordinarily, it was blacker in the shed than a weasel's bedroom.

"What light through yon window breaks?"

Hell's bells, the whole roof had collapsed under the weight of tons of snow and years of service. A great pile of broken timber now reposed in the turntable pit covering the little table. The scene of destruction was clearly visible, illuminated by the rays of the setting sun. The first sunshine to reach this spot in over 40 years. I kicked the snow away from the office doorway, tromped in and sat down in a dusty swivel chair, long unused, put on the headset and twirled the little black crank to alert the dispatcher of my desire to talk.

"Harry," I said, "how is it with you?"

"Warm and sunny down here," he sez, "How is it with you?"

"Bad news, Harry, I'm sitting here in the bay window looking at a hole in the roof; there is a big pile of timber and snow where

Towering Mount Ouray looms over the scene below Shirley Siding, as Rio Grande No. 489 leads a long train of scrap rail down grade off Marshall Pass. The flat bottom gondolas with ends removed to facilitate loading. — JOHN KRAUSE

167

At the left, engineer A. M. Sidenstriker stands beside his Rio Grande narrow-gauge No. 480-class at the west end of the snowshed at Marshall Pass. (RIGHT) The unsung heroes of snow fighting on Marshall Pass were the gandy dancers (trackmen). With nothing more than hand tools, they tackled the iceberg that has stalled a 480-class locomotive. — BOTH S. A. DOUGHERTY

the turntable used to be, and we have the No. 480 crossways to the mouth of the shed with the drag-spreader derailed behind it. The ice is a foot deep inside the snow shed, and you had better figure on a highway move for your cows, as it will take a dozer about a week to clear the tracks and God alone knows how long it will be before we can dig the snow and timber out of the turntable pit so we can turn an engine."

"Thanks, Sam, good luck." he said, and never even offered any helpful suggestions. You see, there was no other traffic involved and a tie-up here did not excite him at all.

Now is where the big men come in. No food since 03:00, 13 hours ago. No carping about when do we eat, they are all down in the snow doing what needs to be done to rerail the equipment and return to Salida before the "hog law" (16 hour service law) gets them.

You can't tell the trainmen or the enginemen from the gandys. They are all shoveling snow, carrying blocks and chains and setting rerailing frogs. In a short time we pulled the spreader back on the iron. Next, the No. 480 was rerailed. Before long we coupled the outfit together and bade farewell to the high lonesome place. I rode the rear platform of the caboose as we backed toward Salida. I was using a big beam, battery powered light to spot any rocks or slides that might have come down after we passed going west that morning. In such a fashion, we crept back to Poncha Junction where we turned on the wye and then slipped into town quietly, arriving about one hour and fifteen minutes on the law. Too late for supper, again!

You will not find a more loyal, dedicated group of railroad men anywhere than the Rio Grande employees who worked on the narrow-gauge.

The Texas cattle were moved by truck and a week later we took a dozer, on a narrow-gauge flatcar, to the top of Marshall Pass where it was unloaded and put to work clearing the ice and snow out of the shed. It took the better part of a week to get the job done. After the CAT operator had finished clearing the half-mile long snowshed he sent for an engine and crew to come haul him home. As soon as the big D-8 CAT was loaded the Roadmaster suggested that the crew run down the track on the west side of the hill and clear a few more miles of snow drifts. Remember, it had been about six weeks since the last train ran over this track, and it was the worst snow period of the year. Well, the first drift encountered west of the portal of the shed was an iceberg big enough to sink the Titanic. When the poor hogger ran into that mass of ice, he stalled. But the brave Roadmaster asked him to back up and take another real good run at it.

The engineer backed into the shed and sanded the rails so the engine would not slip. He opened the throttle wide and came storming out, charging against that frozen mountain of ice. He really gave it his best shot—crunch! Stalled again. Only this time he was not able to back up! The drivers spun and the sparks flew, but she would not budge. The force of the collision had caused the front end plow to bend down, clamping it against the rails. There they stood, stuck fast, unable to move in either direction. The hoghead was nearly in tears to see his pet disabled like that. The four-inch iron bars that supported the wedge were bowed over and the bottom of the plow was hard against the rails. So, now it was time to unload the big cat, pull the caboose back in the shed, tie on

169

Two widths of track gauge at Salida, Colorado. Locomotive No. 1166 was equipped with two couplers to permit handling both standard and narrow-gauge cars. No. 489 had only one coupler for working the "slim" gauge. — JOHN KRAUSE

and slide the little engine backward up the track to where air jacks could be used to bend the twisted iron up enough to clear the rails.

The Master Mechanic was real unhappy with what they had done to his engine. The plow supports had to be taken off, heated red hot, reshaped and then replaced before No. 480 could plow any more snow. And do you know, the Master Maniac blamed the hogger. Said he should have had more sense than to listen to the track monkey, anyhow.

The only time we used the Big Hook to pick up a narrow-gauge engine was when a roundhouse laborer tried to move the little pig without first starting the air pump. The engine was on the turntable lead and the table was lined for the house. When the laborer opened the steam throttle and moved down the track toward the open pit the poor, frightened fellow, unable to stop on account of no air brakes, leaped for safety just as the No. 483 jumped in the hole. That was a long, cold night, I can tell you.

Salida still had a lot of three-rail track that would permit the use of either narrow-gauge or standard gauge cars. Most of the time it worked fine, except on occasion when an old-head crew, called for a Monarch Turn, tried to put one of the slim gauge 'gines up the broad gauge main line right ahead of the *Scenic Limited.* Fortunately we were able to detour the varnish through a yard track and advance the schedule with only a little delay. It took quite a while to coax the little pig back to the proper width of railroad.

When I first went to Salida in December 1952, there were about 500 men working at that busy terminal. We had four or five yard engines assigned, as the narrow-gauge division was hauling coal and limestone. Both of these commodities had to be switched to the barrel transfer for reloading in standard gauge cars. Monarch was going full blast, requiring two trains daily. Salida had a big repair shop where all work on narrow-gauge equipment was done, a shop for off-track equipment repair, and a large storehouse. When I left in 1956 there was only one yard engine working. The shops, repairs and store were gone and the barrel transfer was discontinued. The Marshall Pass line had been abandoned and torn up. The Monarch Branch had been converted to standard gauge. The *Scenic Limited* passenger train that ran through our station had been discontinued. The Big Hook had been moved to Pueblo. I felt like a hatchet man. Of course, all of these decisions were made by higher authority and passed on to the Trainmaster for final execution. All done for the sake of progress and economy.

Trains don't even stop in Salida now. The little slim gauge is no more; rails torn up, buildings razed. Just a few cinders along the weed-grown right-of-way. Mounds of earth piled in long, long graves, housing the ghostly memories of a nearly forgotten age.

The historical records of Rio Grande narrow-gauge disclose very few accidents that involved passenger trains, and only a few major derailments of freight trains. Considering the length of time operated and the number of miles run, the narrow-gauge had an outstanding safety record.

Shaw's Cut on the west side of Marshall Pass was so named to describe the location of a fatal crash that killed engineer Shaw. For some reason, now obscured in the mists of time, a runaway off the top of the 10,860 foot elevation pass ended in a pile of splintered wood and twisted steel. Who knows why? A frozen train line, or perhaps a short brake pipe due to a closed angle cock, or had the hoghead simply "piddled away" his auxiliary reservoir

With all car retaining valves in the heavy holding position, a Rio Grande narrow-gauge 480-class locomotive starts down the 4.5 percent grade out of the Colorado Fuel & Iron limestone quarry at Monarch, Colorado.
— JOHN KRAUSE

pressure by making too frequent applications and releases without sufficient recharge periods? With the ancient equipment then in use, broken brake rods and other brake system failures were often responsible for the loss of train speed control.

There was a runaway on the Monarch Branch in October of 1952. A train load of limestone got out of control as the crew departed the quarry; the 480-class engine and several flat bottom cars turned over about a mile from their initial starting point in the yard. If I recall the facts of that accident correctly, a car toad who worked the trains at Monarch had closed an angle cock in the train line in order to make some repairs to a car brake, and apparently failed to reopen the valve, thereby preventing the engineer from having effective control of his train brakes.

When the runaway reached the highway crossing at high speed, (ten miles per hour was the maximum permissable speed on the 4.5 percent grade) the engineer and fireman went "bird-gang" and got off, landing in a pile of rocks; both men were injured. Rerailing the equipment was a real problem, as the Rio Grande did not have a narrow-gauge derrick in Salida at the time. The ordinary procedure was to scrap and burn the badly damaged cars, and to set a deadman (chev or pulley) whereby a locomotive pulling on a cable was used to retrieve the overturned engine and set it upright. Often a spur track had to be laid to the victim in order to get it back on the iron. In later times, dozers and draglines were employed in narrow-gauge wrecking.

Steam derricks AZ and AO were kept on hand at Alamosa for

protection on Cumbres and the lines running out of the San Luis Valley over Poncha and Marshall passes. Poncha Pass was abandoned and torn up in 1951 and Marshall Pass was closed in 1955.

Wintertime operation, over these high lonesome passes and through the rocky gorges choked with ice and snow, was a frustrating, backbreaking, soul trying endeavor, and fraught with peril. There is no more terrifying experience than a mountain avalanche. Moving at a terrific speed, and with little or no warning, the great weight of snow in motion generates an almost irresistible force, and immovable objects are swept away in its path down the slope; objects such as huge pine trees, giant boulders, houses, railroad track structures, and on occasions, trains.

The ill fated *San Juan* met its destiny at 6:18 P.M. on the 12th of February 1948, when the Toltec Slide came roaring down on the little train as it was inching its way across the nearly perpendicular face of the chasm. Back in 1881 this was the scene of an identical occurrence, which was described in the press as a "particularly gory" accident, when a snow slide swept a passenger train from the rails and into history with 14 passengers and seven deadhead employees killed. Fortunately, the slide of 1948 did not kill anyone, although eleven were injured.

What was probably the most spectacular and least destructive narrow-gauge wreck, was staged in the summer bright meadow of the Animas River Canyon west of Durango on the Silverton Branch in July of 1951. It was a head-on collision between the Nos. 462 and 473, and was perpetrated before several movie cameras in an important sequence of the motion picture *Denver and Rio Grande.* To get the realistic, big bang effect, the pilots and front ends of the engines, both obsolete, scrap heap candidates, were loaded with dynamite and other pyrotecnics. When all systems were go, the crews fired up their engines, hot and smoking, released the brakes, opened the steam throttles wide, and got off as the exhaust thundered from the stacks of the opposing trains. They charged at one another like rutting rams, and plowed together with a mighty roar that echoed from the high vermillion cliffs of the deep gorge.

During my tour of narrow-gauge duty, there were some

Rio Grande No. 268, often called "Cinderella," steams up to pull the last train load of cows out of Iola, Colorado, on the Sapinero Branch during September 1953. Engineer Frank B. Wright was at the throttle. — JOHN KRAUSE

The very last train from Sapinero. The No. 268 makes a lot of black smoke as she pulls the house track for the final time. Old railroad men and rail enthusiasts were on hand to witness the sad event. — JOHN KRAUSE

memorable "lasts." I was Trainmaster at Salida when we operated the last stock special out of the Gunnison Valley. In days long past, the movement of the Iola Pool was an exciting event; four or five owners of the large cattle ranches would round up their herds and cut out the beautiful animals destined for the eastern packing houses. Together they formed the "Pool." It took the No. 268, working overtime, to haul the empty stock cars from Gunnison to the chutes at Iola, and there the cowboys pushed their reluctant doggies to the first step of becoming hamburger on the hoof. Generally a carnival atmosphere prevailed, with a good deal of celebrating, and rodeo type antics from the high spirited punchers. I'm sorry to say that the last round up was very subdued. Perhaps they all realized that this was the final performance, the end of an era in ranching, and in railroading. This grim fact seemed to dampen their spirits.

To handle the move we brought two 480-class engines and a train crew into Gunnison with the empties. My old duck hunting buddy, and onetime fellow local chairman, Frank B. Wright, was in charge of the faithful No. 268. We took the train to Iola, loaded the herd and chuffed sadly back to the terminal on his last trip that memorable day. Two additional 480-class engines had been called out of Salida to help the train from Sargent to Marshall Pass. They refueled and filled their cisterns at the station and waited for our train of stock. In short order we cut the helpers in the swing, and were highballing for Shawano Tank and the shed at the top of the hill. The helpers were cut out of the train at the summit for our descent.

The Salida yardmaster had called in an extra goat to expedite the transfer at Cleora stock yards, and a Pueblo road crew was called for the special train which got out way ahead of schedule. In less than 16 hours the fat cows, of the last Iola Pool, reached the market in Denver. Exceptionally good time we were told, but no one felt much like celebrating.

I rode the last train of Rio Grande equipment out of Gunnison. We had taken a train of wooden flat bottom coal cars which had their ends removed to facilitate scrap loading, to the contractor. He was putting the finishing touches on a masterpiece of railroad history . . . abandonment. Then picking up the remnants of a broken dream, we gathered a train of stock cars for our final trip

Rio Grande locomotive No. 489, in service for the contractor, was hired to dismantle the Gunnison Branch in May 1955. — JOHN KRAUSE

to Salida.

A goodly number of rail enthusiasts had secured passes to ride along on the last run, which occurred May 2, 1955. Storm clouds hung low over the mountain peaks named for Chief Ouray and his wife, Chipeta. An early spring snow storm was eminent, so before we got under way, I had the yardmaster put on a deadhead caboose to provide the rail buffs with a warm, dry place to ride and keep their camera and sound equipment out of the weather. Some of these men had come from as far away as Connecticut to ride this train. It was a sorrowful bunch, I might add, all of them knew this was the end of an exciting chapter in railroad history. A gloomy day of clouds, mists and intermittent snow squalls made good photography difficult.

The "last" revenue shipment over the famous third division was an electrical monstrosity destined for the new power station being built in Gunnison. It was a huge transformer that taxed all of our published clearances en route. It arrived in Salida loaded on a special type of "well" flatcar, one with a lowered center section and extra journals to bear the tremendous weight. Using the Big Hook we made the transfer to a narrow-gauge flatcar. Once loaded on that tiny car, it loomed high above the caboose and was as wide as the car. It looked so top-heavy I doubted we could even get it out of the yard without turning it over.

Within two hours of departure from the terminal, disaster struck . . . the big load had derailed. We called the carmen out of Salida to go by truck to the scene of the trouble, in the canyon below Mear's Junction, to rerail the valuable shipment. By the time they arrived, the conductor and his two helpers had rerailed it by themselves, using a rerailing frog and some hardwood wedges from the caboose. I instructed the car toads to drive along the highway, which ran parallel with the track as far as the Junction, just in case.

Night fell and I went to bed, but it was a fitful rest. So, I got up at around 04:00 and drove over Monarch Pass to Sargent, arriving just as the courageous little train hove 'round the bend. Trouble? Yes, some, the crew explained as I drove them to a cafe for breakfast. They had been off the track seven times! With each derailment handled like the first, by themselves. I followed the train on into Gunnison. En route it derailed two more times. Low wheels, low rails, and low speeds make for fairly simple "off-again-on-again-gone-again-Finnigan." Old head conductors know how. More of little engines and big men.

The transformer arrived safely and was delivered on site in good condition, and in less than 16 hours. I was glad that we did not have to make a delivery like that every day.

I was there for the last narrow-gauge train out of Monarch, and I was there to ride the first standard gauge train of lime rock through the Garfield Switchback. One chapter finished, a new chapter begun.

Westbound Rio Grande freight train No. 33, pulled by L-131 Mallet-type No. 3609, gains the crest of the Continental Divide at Tennessee Pass. Colorado's Mount Elbert, 14,431 feet high, is at the right. — R. H. KINDIG

12

Runaway On Minturn Hill

T*HE RAILROAD* tunnel at Tennessee Pass is 2,500 feet long where it burrows through the crest of the Continental Divide. With an elevation of 10,242 feet it is the highest standard gauge railroad in the United States. Westward trains emerging from the west portal, now on the Pacific watershed, enter a three percent grade for 21 miles to Minturn, Colorado. The engineer who views this scene for the first time is reminded of looking down from the ridgepole of a steep roof. It is no place for faint hearts or weak minds. Here is where the schoolboys are separated from the masters. To railroad men it is the famed Minturn Hill. Successful train handlers recognize an old axiom: "Keep the speed low and the air brake pressure high."

I can still see those great, black Mallets leading long trains of cars obscured by blue smoke from hundreds of scorched wheels; brake shoes worn thin and hot enough to fry eggs on them. In the old days the trainmen walked the tops of the freight cars to put up the "pops" on all westward trains. (Pressure retaining valves were called "pops.") When the valve handles were placed in the heavy holding position 20 pounds of brake cylinder pressure was

On September 25, 1938 the third section of train No. 2 ran as an American Legion Special between Los Angeles and New York City. No. 1516 on the point assists No. 1712 as both locomotives put power to the rail on the three percent grade at Rex, Colorado. — GERALD M. BEST

Minturn, Colorado, as it looked during the great age of the steam locomotive. No. 3600 has just taken on coal and water, moved up to the ready track, and waits for a helper assignment on the big hill. - GERALD M. BEST

retained in the cylinder to keep the brakes applied while the brake pipe and auxiliary reservoir pressure was being restored.

Several runaways occurred on this subdivision, and while I was never involved in one, I did have a shocking incident with the Big Hook. Honest, we let the damn thing get away from us. Not just once, but twice! Any fool can make a mistake once, but to pull the same dumb stunt again borders on idiocy! Here's what happened. Those old stump pullers were equipped with air brakes, but not hand brakes. I guess they were afraid someone would leave the binder on and drag the wheels flat. To tie the derrick down you had to block the wheels, or better still, leave the machine coupled to its boom car, which had a double hand brake.

The first instance of losing the derrick went like this. We had gone to Americus Siding to retruck a car of ore that had suffered a burned off journal—hot box gone too long. After getting the head end of the eastward freight train in the clear we took the Big Hook up against the crippled car. We raised it high enough to put a skid tie under the west truck and could then slide the car down the main track. Next we got the freight train recoupled and sent it on its way to Salida. Now we were faced with the task of taking the damaged truck out from under the hopper car of ore and replacing it with a new truck. As the derrick was trained west of its boom car and the bad order wheels were on the west end of the hopper, we had to cut the Hook away from its tender. That let us swing the boom around so we could make a lift on the west end of the disabled car once we had switched the machine into position. Ordinarily the switching job should have been done by running around the car through the siding. The Superintendent wanted to save a few minutes so he suggested we cut the derrick away from the boom car and use the walking gear to move over the west switch and then walk the big machine down grade against the cripple. All well and good, she moved away from her tender, over the switch, and then came east on the main track. As the derrick moved along side the boom car it stopped to pick up a new truck and then proceeded walking east toward the disabled car.

All of a sudden the little walking gear stripped! "Kerrr-thrrrip." The ponderous machine starting running downgrade toward the standing car of ore, holding the swinging pair of wheels from her boom line. There was no hand brake to set; the air had been bled from her brake cylinders to make the move. Faster, faster, it went with about 15 car lengths to run. The Car Foreman leaped to safety from the poop deck, right over my back as I ran alongside trying to get a wooden block under the wheels of the runaway. "BA-LOOMMM." The derrick engineer dropped the suspended wheels on the top of the car of ore "Ka-plunk" amid a great cloud of dust. No damage, except to the nervous systems and egos. Just too damn close. I swore an oath that was the "last" time I would ever be a party to separating 150 tons of freewheeling Big Hook from a good hand brake.

Well, the "last" time we lost it was at Redcliff and here's what happened. I'll start from the beginning. It was the opening day of the elk season and I had a few days vacation time coming. I had made plans to go hunting near Princeton; bought new boots, a red shirt and was all dressed to leave for the high country about 04:00, when the phone rang. The Chief Dispatcher wanted me to take a deadhead crew to Howard to relieve a Pueblo crew that had run out of time (the hog law got them). Yes, I agreed to help him out; postponing my trip for an hour or two. All decked out for the the hills, I drove to the office where I received the flash of a new development. The *WPF*, an eastbound fruit block had sideswiped some derailed reefers in a westbound freight drag at the Twin Bridges, just west of the Red Cliff station.

Forget the elk hunting, forget the deadhead crew. Just get on your horse and try to get a line on what was necessary to clear the railroad. I called the Salida Hook, and ordered "Samson de Grande" from the west. My first count was 27 cars piled up, blocking both main lines. Get going!

Well, about three days later, I was hobbling around on badly blistered feet, still in those damn new boots and red shirt, trying to pick up the last of the derailment.

We had spotted the Big Hook, from Grand Junction, on the westbound main just west of the crossover and tied it down, ready to make a lift. We were going to raise and retruck a car when someone suggested cutting the Salida Hook away from its tender and using the walking gear to move the machine through the crossover from the eastbound track into a working position on the westbound, upgrade from where old Samson was parked. I at once vetoed the move, recalling the sorry performance at Americus. I

"Up on the boom, down on the light line." Rio Grande derrick No. 028 goes to work clearing the main track at Tennessee Pass on a July day in 1956. — S. A. DOUGHERTY

Known as *Sampson de Grande*, derrick No. 028 swings its boom around to tackle a pileup at Tennessee Pass. — S. A. DOUGHERTY

Built Narrow Gage to Malta in 1880, to Rock Creek (M.P. 296.74) in 1881 and to Minturn in 1887.
" 3-Rail " " " 1890, Standard Gage in 1925.
Standard Gage - Malta to Minturn in 1890.
Second Track built Rex (M.P. 298.00) to Minturn in 1903.
" " " Red Cliff to Rex in 1907.
" " " Pando to Red Cliff in 1909
" " " Deen (M.P. 286.78) to Pando 10-22-1910
" " " East Mitchell (M.P. 281.96) to West Mitchell (M.P. 284.57) in 1928.
Block Signal System Installed - Salida to Minturn in 1928.
" " " " " M.P. 214.60 to 215.37 in 1942.
C.T.C. M.P. 280.00 to 286.79 Installed in 1928
" Installed - Kobe to Tennessee Pass in 1958.
" " - Deen to Minturn in 1958.
" " - Salida to Kobe in 1961.
" " - W. Salida to E. Salida in 1967.

This track profile map of Tennessee Pass is like looking down from a roof top. With an eastward grade of three percent and maximum curvature of 12 degrees, Minturn Hill was a tough 86.91 miles of mountain railroading during the era of steam. — COURTESY OF THE DENVER & RIO GRANDE WESTERN RAILROAD

184

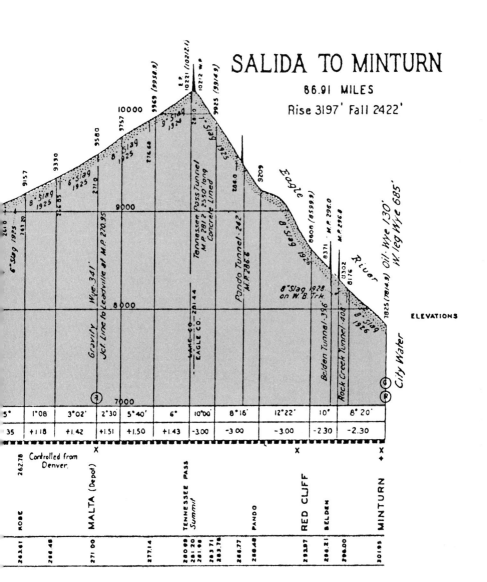

SALIDA TO MINTURN

86.91 MILES

Rise 3197' Fall 2422'

ELEVATIONS

Machines to match the mountains. Rio Grande No. 3610 fills the canyon with coal smoke and the echoing sound of exhaust as she roars over the Eagle River bridge west of Minturn, Colorado. — DONALD DUKE

was overruled. As soon as the coupling pin was lifted she moved about three feet, stripping her gears again! It then shot down that three percent grade like a cannon ball. With her boom high and lined to the left, she flew toward the stationary "Samson de Grande." There was no stopping her. The Salida derrick engineer swung the boom hard right just as the collision occurred. I can still see the picture of those two upright, steel booms slapping against one another like long necked dinosaurs locked in deadly combat, iron ringing on iron, echoing through the narrow confines of that rocky gorge.

I could not move. I was petrified with fear, sure we had killed somebody in the collision. There had been a number of carmen and section men working in the area. Luckily, no one was injured. The only damage was to the draft gear on the front of the derricks. I could just visualize those two giant machines turned over on their sides in the Eagle River. How in the hell could you ever explain that to your boss? The poor Car Foreman was as scared as I was; after the crash he nearly passed out. Pale as a fish's belly, he sat down on the rail shivering and shaking. We were both afraid to see the damage and were very relieved to learn there were no fatalities. I swore again. Never, ever, would anyone talk me into walking the Big Hook under its own power. But shortly after this unfortunate incident, and as a result of our experience, the company took the walking gear off the derricks. As many times as I went out with the outfit after that "last" time, I never permitted anyone to pull the pin between the derrick and its boom car. I had some hot words with Superintendents and Trainmasters, but never again did I fall for that sucker play. Two chances were all I ever took! I figured it was one more than I was entitled to.

A trip over the line between Minturn and Tennessee Pass is filled with memories of many derailments that occurred at points along the way. Two separate accidents, at the west switch Pando Siding, each involved 19 cars of an eastbound freight train. During my tenure as Trainmaster at Salida we did a lot of experimentation on where to train the diesel helping power. It was during the transition period from steam to diesel helpers that we had to learn how much tonnage to put ahead of the swing helper and how much behind. We made some mistakes. Most of

Heading for the Moffat Tunnel, this giant L-131 class 2-8-8-2 type locomotive blackens the Colorado blue sky near milepost 47, east of Tolland Siding, as she blasts her way up the two percent grade. — R. H. KINDIG

The D&RGW had 14 of these sleek speedsters built by the Baldwin Locomotive Works in 1929. Numbered 1700 through 1713, these Northern type 4-8-4's developed 64,000 pounds tractive effort. They carried 240 psi working steam pressure, had 27x30-inch cylinders, and 70-inch drivers. They were used principally in passenger service. The author logged a lot of miles as a fireman on these beautiful machines. — GERALD M. BEST

Numbered 1800 through 1804, these Baldwin built Northern type engines had 73-inch drivers, carried 285 psi working steam pressure and developed 68,000 pounds tractive effort. The tender had a 20,000 gallon water capacity and held 28 tons of coal. These were the pride of the Rio Grande's passenger fleet. Received in 1937, they turned in many miles until replaced by diesels in 1953. The author fired this long-legged, high-wheeler for his father on train No. 5, the *Exposition Flyer.* Down through the Utah Valley at 80 mph, she rode like a baby buggy. — GERALD M. BEST

189

Rio Grande No. 3100 leads a fast freight westbound at Snowden, Colorado. Snowden is a wide spot on the railroad south of Leadville. — FRED SCHNEIDER

these resulted in broken couplers that fell into the center of the track, and with the rear helper pushing a few cars off before it could stop. Too much horsepower on the head end was always good for a break-in-two at the point of vertical curve at Pando Flat. "Flat," that is where the grade breaks from a three percent to a 0.0 for a short distance and then ascends to a 1.5 percent for a mile before resuming the heavy grade again. The big horses on the head end would gallop off and leave their trailing tonnage as soon as the locomotive and head cars hit the lighter grade and all of that pulling power was suddenly transformed to speed.

We also had some overspeed (coupling above normal speed) impacts. Once when recoupling a train at Tennessee Pass after cutting out the swing helper, and the road engine hoghead, backing up blind, groping for the joint, came back too fast and collided with his stationary rear end. All of that weight and momentum had to suddenly change from vertical movement to a lateral movement or go straight up. Usually it just turned the rails over under the cars in the "jackknifing" action. And unless someone (trainman) noticed the displaced rails, any further movement resulted in several rails being turned over and more cars derailed. Then we would have another call for the Big Hook. We had a lot of this type of accident until we finally cured it (in part, at least) with a new Operating Rule No. 102-D:

"In the event of a rough coupling or harsh slack action, incidental to stopping cars or trains, inspection must be made of the locomotive, cars and track. It must be determined whether any equipment has been damaged or rails displaced as a result of jackknifing action between the locomotive units or cars in that portion liable to damage. Inspection must be made on each side of the locomotive and cars and it must be known that the track and equipment are in a safe condition before proceeding."

Many new rules had to be written and old rules revised to properly provide safety for employees, track and equipment. the diesel locomotive created nearly as many problems as it solved.

One of the three most poignant memories I have of the Big Hill is when three L-131 class Mallets, they were the 3600's, filled the world with sound as they blasted their stacks upgrade through the narrow canyon between Rex and Red Cliff. What a roar they made! Black smoke boiling and billowing and a rain of cinders falling. When one of those old girls slipped her drivers, everything in the cab jumped up and down and shook loose. You had to be there! There are no words to adequately describe what it was like, with the noise, the smells, and the feeling you got from being there.

We ran wrecker trains and snow plows; fought slides and high water, wash outs and wash ins, and in all that four and one half year period we never had a fatality or a serious personal injury to an employee on the Salida district. Of that fact I am very proud and happy. The Trainmaster himself got hurt worse than anyone when he damn near got run over one snowy day at Pando.

The Ford Train is the hottest of the hotshot freight trains on the Rio Grande. Here No. 3101 west, drifts across the flat at Pando Siding, Colorado, in 1976. — RON C. HILL

13

Close Call at Pando

WHEN THE Rocky Mountains were formed, a great upheaval of granite rock and earth was split apart by a tremendous force. This action created a wide rift which eroded into a broad valley around 9,000 feet elevation. Shallow lakes were formed and filled with the pure water from winter snow. It was on these lakes that the railroad crews cut and harvested ice for company use. The winters in these mountains are long and cold and at Pando the snow piles deep. The U.S. Army built a camp at Pando for training troops who were to serve in the Alps of Italy and in the Aleutian Islands during World War II. Cooper Hill remains a popular ski course to this day. Now open to the public, the course was originally built as an adjunct to the Army's winter training program.

During the construction period most of the building material was brought to Camp Pando by rail. A long spur track was laid into the camp area, and for lack of a better name it was called the Government Track. When the war ended the camp was abandoned. By 1954 only a few of the old barracks and the spur line were all that remained of the original installation. It was here the Army reestablished a camp to train mountain troops for possible service in Korea, and this is where I had a very, very close call. This is what happened.

It was early February and snow lay deep in the Rockies when we got word of a troop train out of Fort Carson at Colorado Springs bound for Pando. No train movement had been made over the Government Track in months and ice covered the rails into the camp area. I instructed the Roadmaster to have his section men clean all of the switches connected with the movement. The track was a west end connected spur, which meant that our train, coming from Colorado Springs and heading west from Pueblo, would come down the westbound main line at Pando. It would then pull west of the switch to the spur track and back the troop sleepers into the camp where Army vehicles could drive and unload the soldiers.

As Trainmaster-Road Foreman it was my duty to ride the troop train out of Salida to Pando. My function was to expedite the movement and see that all went well, maintaining rules and safety as well as operation of the equipment.

We had a picked crew on that cold and frosty morning, leaving at daybreak. Earl Roberts was the hoghead with "Smiley" Earl Flynn as his fireman. Old Missouri Stewart was the conductor and two fine lads, "Slick" Haley and Jimmy Allen were the brakemen.

The train got out of Salida on schedule and the four big EMD units literally flew up the grade having only twelve trailing coaches. Roberts promptly put me to work as he knew how I liked (loved) to run an engine and handle a train. What a thrill to feel all of that horsepower and to see the beautiful winterscape of the majestic Collegiate Range; to look back at the long sweep of the train on the curves with the fine snow billowing from beneath the coaches. Not many working men are so privileged. After a stop at Tennessee Pass we dropped on down the ten miles of three percent grade to Pando Flat. I thanked Roberts for letting me exercise my skills and got off at the Government Track switch. I wanted to be on the rear end for the ride into the camp.

Roberts took over his engineer's duties and pulled the train westward, over the switch and prepared to back into the unloading area. There was about four feet of snow on the level and it was twelve feet high where the section men had piled what they had

194

Rio Grande's No. 179 west, the Ford Train at Redcliff, Colorado, in 1976. Now a single track line, and equipped with Centralized Traffic Control, old Minturn Hill is just not the same. — RON C. HILL

cleaned from around the switch stand. This high snow, piled so close to the track, almost got me killed.

Allen lined the gate (switch), gave the hogger a backup signal, and swung aboard the first open vestibule. Roberts was moving slowly back. Stewart got on and when I took hold of the grab irons on the coach and stepped up with my trailing foot first, the slick composition sole of my right shoe slipped off the step! I tried to pull myself up but my left shin came down on the iron tread just as our eastward movement dragged me, still clinging with both hands from the hand irons, into the twelve foot high pile of frozen snow east of the switch. There was not room enough to clear my protruding rear end, and as the movement continued, my body was rotated, and turned backward. My left arm was separated from its shoulder socket and the dragging movement broke my right hand grasp. I fell, rolling off the snow pile, down—toward the rail. I ended up lying parallel with the track on the ends of the crossties, my face against the cold steel rail and my right ear inches from those rolling, clicking, moving wheels! My whole life did not flash before me. My only conscious thought was to lie still, flatten out, and if I moved, not to place my arm over that rail as it would surely get cut off!

Once, while working as a fireman out of Grand Junction I had been an eyewitness to a fatality when the No. 1189 ran over a Yardmaster. I recalled this event all too vividly and I did not want to end up a pile of steaming, bloody rags like he did. So I laid very still and quiet as five coaches passed over me. I could feel the bottoms of the car journal boxes brushing my back and I prayed to God that nothing was hanging down to catch on my clothes and start me rolling along with those clicking wheels. You can talk all you want about your nightmares, but many is the time since that incident that I have awakened in a cold sweat. Even now, writing about this it makes my gut churn. Frankly, I'd rather not think about it at all, thanks!

Old "Mo" Stewart saw me fall and he went racing through the coach aisle, packed with soldiers, trying to get to an emergency valve. Five cars had rolled over me before I heard the welcome blast of compressed air when the brake pipe was reduced to zero and iron clamped on iron to stop the clickety-clack in my ears. Even after the stop I was afraid to move. Still on my belly, I tried to get my right hand under me in order to raise up on my knees and back myself out of there. I guessed I was about six or eight feet east of the cleared area around the switch, as I could see only dim light because the snow had packed behind the lens of my glasses. My left arm was useless and dangling limply. It hurt like hell. I could hear Missouri Stewart calling, "Sam? Sam . . . are you all right?" in a kind of tenuous tone of voice, like he really didn't expect me to answer. And was he ever relieved and grinning all over when he saw me crab-crawling, rear end first, out of that cramped space beside the rail. He was as pale as milk and so were the two brakemen. They helped me aboard the train and we backed into the camp. There were Army medics on the train, but because of some dumb Army Regulation, they could do nothing to ease the pain or give me any kind of relief. I was a civilian. So there I sat, nursing my dislocation for over an hour while the troops were being unloaded. They finally sent a Jeep to bring me to the camp hospital where an Army doctor layed me on a table and had two GI's hold me while he rotated and pulled on my arm. When that joint slipped back in its socket, I swear I never felt anything so good. I wore an Army sling for a few days and went on with my regular duties.

You can bet the first thing I did was to order a dozer to clear the piles of snow from around the switches at every point on the subdivision where snow was deep enough to make a pile. There was no reason to take any more chances. I figured I had used all of our good luck.

It was a long time before I felt just right about getting on or off moving equipment. Not only does pride go with a fall, confidence goes as well.

Several years later I happened to be in Salida on company business and ran into "Mo" Stewart in a grocery store. I went up to him and said,

"Hello, Mo. Do you remember me? I'm Sam Dougherty."

He was way past 80 years old, I know. He had a hearing aid in each ear, but he heard me and tears came in his old, faded blue eyes. He choked, smiled and said,

"Hell yes, I remember you. You are the guy we ran over at Pando and scared me half to death. I've thought about that day many times. Boy, I am sure glad to see you."

We visited for a while and I left him to do his shopping. He had been retired for ten years or so then. I read in the paper a year later that he had died. He was a fine old man, a damn good railroad man, and if he had a given name I never heard it. Maybe it was Missouri, shortened to "Mo." One more colorful chapter of my experiences on the "high iron."

In 1979 Rio Grande extra No. 5335 east wheels a drag of empty coal hoppers by the towering portal of the Castle Gate, in Utah. — RON C. HILL

14

Anything Can Happen

ALL TRAIN derailments are serious, of course, many were tragic, and several were spectacular. They were as varied as the people, the scenes, and the events. All of my memories crowd for recognition.

My job was one that left little time for boredom. Each trip was different, every experience a challenge. Seldom if ever were they not exciting and interesting. Like the big pileup at Woodside back in 1962.

A 100-car fast freight train left Helper at midnight, rolling eastward. Within an hour of its departure 39 of those cars were stacked up in a huge heap of twisted metal and splintered wood at the west siding switch. A wheel broke just east of Grassy Siding and ran, undetected by the crew, until it crossed the frog of the switch and went out in the river. At 50 m.p.h. there is a lot of momentum to dissipate. All of the derailed cars were tightly packed within a distance of 200 feet!

I was in Helper when it happened and rode out with the Big Hook to the scene. It was a monumental mess! Cars were scattered like jackstraws, upside down, broken open and lading

No. 3096 leads a train of piggyback and auto rack cars on train No. 136, as it rolls eastward out of Helper, Utah. — RON C. HILL

strewn among the wreckage. In the center of the pile were two big, high, auto box cars, both off their trucks, sitting side by side. Perched on top of them, standing on one end and leaning at a 45 degree angle was the deck of a flatcar. That car was supporting a big, red Santa Fe box car which was standing on one end and tilted so that it looked like a gigantic "A-frame," looming high above the tangled wreckage. On the side doors and on each end of the AT&SF car were bright red placards that declared in bold letters "EXPLOSIVE Rocket Propellant." There it sat, perched on top of the two cars, leaning on a third, sticking up over 60 feet in the air, silhouetted against the desert sky.

There was no possible way to move the cars without risking an explosion. All we could do was work around it until the inspector from the Bureau of Explosives arrived to examine the "high-bust" load. When he finally did show up and saw the position of the dangerous car he remarked,

"Well, I could tell you how to clear this entire mess, but I can't tell you where to get enough dirt to fill the crater that thing would create if it blew up."

The explosives expert used a long ladder and some ropes to get into a position where he could open the box car door and examine the contents. He gave a great sigh of relief upon finding no damage to the cannisters and said it would be "OK" to move the car. We then simply attached a winch line from a big D-8 CAT and gave the low end of the car a pull; it slid down from its precarious perch into the soft sand along the river with hardly a bump. No one took a deep breath until it was down.

There is a great amount of just plain, pure, dumb luck involved in the things that happen on a railroad. When you have looked at many scenes of devastation and destruction you can nearly always say, "Well, it could have been worse." Like the time we lost the rear unit of a helper locomotive under the worst possible conditions. It ran away down hill for two miles at high speed, jumped the track and disappeared into a stand of jack pines without leaving a trace! It ended up so far from the railroad we had to bulldoze a roadway in order to drag it back to the right-of-way in order to retruck the damn thing.

Here is essentially what happened. An eastbound coal train, of about 70 cars, came out of Moffat County with five big GP-30's on the point. They stopped at Tabernash to pick up a two unit helper behind the caboose for the assault on Fraser Hill. The hill is four miles of two percent grade west of the big bore at the Moffat Tunnel. A lot of queer things can happen on a railroad. My father used to say,

"Anything can happen on a railroad and it usually does, and it will be at the worst possible time."

An early day version of Murphy's Law, no doubt. Sometimes I think that Murphy proposed his law as a result of his railroad experience!

Just before the big train reached the apex in the tunnel, at 9,500

No. 3109, an EMD GP40-2 built in 1972, gives an eastbound coal liner a boost up Fraser Hill at Hideaway Park, Colorado. — RON C. HILL

feet elevation, the air brakes applied in emergency and everything came to a grinding halt. And there they sat in the pitch blackness and smoke. What in hell had caused this interruption? The conductor and rear brakeman grabbed their hand lanterns, a new air hose, an alligator wrench, and got off the caboose at its east end. A serious mistake in this case, but one commonly made by train crews who automatically exclude the rear helper engine and crummy when they start out to look for trouble. The two men made their way forward to the head end of the train without finding a ruptured hose or broken brake pipe. There is very little clearance alongside the rails in the Moffat Tunnel, and the huge fan at the east end blew all of the exhaust smoke from the road engine back in their faces.

The engineer and fireman on the helper engine just sat there in the dark and the smoke, and neither of them got down on the ground to inspect their machinery; thereby overlooking the cause of all of the trouble.

The front end air hose between the leading helper unit and the caboose had looped down far enough to rub on the rock plow (pilot) of the GP-30. It rubbed and chafed then finally wore a hole in the tough rubberized material. "POW," the pressure blew an even bigger hole and the brake pipe reduced to atmosphere. It made for a real rough stop, as the resulting slack action broke the knuckle in the coupler between the two units. This separated them by several feet, pulling out the control jumpers and breaking the main reservoir supply pipe. When the control circuit on the rear unit was lost the diesel engine "konked out," thereby stopping the air compressor. The air pressure in the brake system reduced to zero through the main reservoir supply line. So there she sat in the dark, dead and powerless. Soon the Law of Gravity manifested itself. The roller bearing axles started to rotate on the slightly descending grade . . . westward.

Swiftly the unit ran, faster and faster as the speed increased on the one percent grade. When she reached the two percent just west of the east switch at Winter Park she really took off! The train dispatcher at his console in Denver saw the track light indicator flash on when the runaway crossed the switch at that location. Forty seconds later the indicator at the west switch came on to show that the track there was occupied. That siding is one-mile long! Whatever had activated his circuits was sure as hell moving, he noted as he alerted the Chief. Lucky there were no closely following movements. Whoops! The track lights between Winter Park and Fraser went out. The circuits showed clear, unoccupied. Nothing!

Around this same time the conductor of the stalled train worked his way back to his caboose and discovered that they had lost a unit! He contacted the Chief Dispatcher immediately to report the runaway. The control center put out a call for the section forces to start patrolling their districts to find the escapee or any track damage it might have caused in its flight. A Section Foreman and a Roadmaster both passed the lost unit without seeing it, being so well hidden, concealed by jack pines. It never left a mark at the point where it became airborne. That massive piece of machinery traveled over two hundred feet from the right-of-way!

The *California Zephyr*, train No. 17 westbound at the South Boulder Creek bridge (milepost 48), between Tolland and East Portal, Colorado. — RON C. HILL

15

The Free Riders

N O TRAIN wreck could ever be called funny, however, some humor has evolved along the way. Like the time we headed in at Granby on the East Pass to meet a westbound hotshot. It was a scorching hot day in August and the mosquitos were boiling out of the swamps. We got a green dwarf signal and started out of the siding. As we picked up speed to 30 m.p.h. and waited for a "highball" from the conductor to resume track speed we heard a frantic call on the train radio,

"Stop the train! We're in the ditch!"

Then the air went in the "bighole," POW! and the train ground to a screeching halt. Holy smoke, what now? The head shack and I got off and started back along the train, fighting clouds of insects as we looked for the trouble. We found it, too. Thirteen cars were involved, having either turned over, jackknifed, or off their trucks, but none were too badly damaged; about 35 rail lengths of track had been torn up with rail sections displaced and ties chewed up.

The blistering hot sun had caused the siding to "run" or sun-kink, just as our rear end came off the east switch. When rails get hot they expand and that expansion creates a terrific amount of energy that must be expended. It has got to go somewhere, so it kicks the whole track structure off the grade. I have witnessed a couple of these "runs" in the past. The rails and ties just lift up out of the ballast and move laterally four or five feet, bending 110 pound rail like it was cooked spaghetti!

One of the duties of a supervisor is to get a good and accurate picture of the car and track damage at the scene of a derailment. This information is then passed along to the powers at headquarters. They require car numbers, lading, damage, position in the pileup and so forth. As I was walking back toward the rear end of the train I took out my pocket notebook to draw a sketch of the scene and grab car numbers. Just about half way to the rear I met two transients, both of whom were more than half full of tequila, and who were weaving their way alongside the wrecked equipment.

Our dialogue was as follows:

"Hey, boddy, wen you gonna run de tren?"

"Hell, man, I don't know. We've got trouble." I went right on copying car numbers.

"Hey, boddy, we wan to go to Denber."

"Christ, man, were you riding in one of these wrecked cars?" I asked.

"Hey, boddy, chew shu see wher we was ridin."

"Were either of you hurt?" I wanted to know if we had a case for a doctor's attention.

"No, we don' get hur', we are hokay."

So I went on walking and writing numbers. They followed, watching me write.

"Hey, boddy, neber min' de nummers, les run de tren." was his parting shot.

That phrase became a popular by-line whenever anyone got too involved in paper work and numbers. "Hey, boddy, neber min' de nummers, les run de tren!"

When our General Manager arrived at the scene of the wreck, the first thing he did was to hike off to the village and returned carrying an armful of mosquito repellent. He gave each man his own individual spray can for protection. It was damn near impossible to work in the swarms of insects thirsting for our blood.

We had a funny thing happen once as a result of finding some drunken hobos in the rear cab of a locomotive that was pulling a westbound hotshot out of Denver. I was riding the train to check the schedule which was pretty fast. As soon as we cleared the yard I went from the head end back over the five-unit consist checking engine loading, oil, air pressures and general operating efficiency of the engine. It was just dusk when I opened the cab door of the last unit and at once realized it was occupied. I snapped on my flashlight and there in its beam I saw bodies sprawled on the floor and in the cab seats. Five free riders. All passed out, their empty gallon jug sitting in the center of the whole mess.

Well, hell! I sure hated to delay this important train to unload these winos and still, I didn't want them there either. Five of them would be a pretty big load for me to handle alone. Really, they were too drunk to unload out there on the mountain; and they'd probably kill themselves trying to get back on the train, anyway, so I left them alone. I threw the jug off as I made my way back to the head end. As soon as I arrived in the operating unit I called the Chief Dispatcher on the radio and ask him to alert the county sheriff at Granby and to have him meet our train at the station. We pulled into the little town and three deputies took charge of my hung over buddies.

About a month after the incident I met one of the county cops at Winter Park and he sure took me on for the trouble I had caused. He was mad as hell! It seems those 'bos I unloaded on him had lice and the police were having trouble debugging their jail!

Free riders were always a source of trouble. They were frequently involved in accidents; getting themselves killed or cut up. The law forbids a common carrier to haul passengers without charging the required tariff. Many 'bos rode in spite of the best effort by the railroad police to prevent it. During the depression years the hobos rode trains by the hundred. In my home town of Helper, every train that stopped unloaded what looked like an army of traveling men.

I walked into a dark cab one cold, wintery night in Fraser Canyon only to find it occupied by two fine gentlemen who needed a ride to Salt Lake City. They were friendly types and I did not have the heart to stop the train and put them off in the snow. They

Rio Grande train No. 788, a coal liner east at Pando, Colorado. Eighteen units handle 10,000 tons in 99 hoppers on the three percent grade between Minturn and Tennessee Pass. — RON C. HILL

would have frozen to death in the sub-zero weather, so I let them ride along but warned them not to go poking around in the high voltage lockers and getting themselves fried like an egg. Somewhat of an exaggeration, but effective, nonetheless.

That experience brings to mind an old story of what happened to "Stutterin Bill" O'Brien one time when he was firing a passenger train on the desert. Bill had gone back on the engine cistern to take water at Green River and had found a big, burley hobo in the doghouse. Now, most all steam engines except the later models with the vestibule cabs had a "Chic Sale" sized cabin built on top of the tank where the head brakeman of freight crews could get in out of the weather. There were only two seats on those older steam engines, one for the hoghead and one for the fireman. On a passenger train the head shack could ride inside the coach with the people. Anyway, when Bill threw the tank spout around after filling the tank, he got back in the cab and told his engineer about the free rider. This old "eagle eye" was a hard boiled dude and he made life miserable for student firemen, trainmen and especially hobos, so he says;

"Bill, go back and throw the bastard off!" And Bill went back as instructed. He returned soon.

"Did you unload the S.O.B.?" the hogger wanted to know.

"Naw, hell, he ain't a bad fella'. Let him ride." says Bill, only stammering on fffella'.

"Bull Shit!" roared the old crab. "I'll put that bastard off!" He jumped down off his seat and away he went, climbed up on the tank and flung open the door of the doghouse to look square into the muzzle of a big .44 held by the occupant. He climbed right down, got on the engine, mounted his throne and whistled off, waiting for a signal.

"DDDDid yyyou unload hhhim?" asked Bill.

"You know, Bill, you were right. He is really a nice fella', so I let him ride. He ain't doin' no harm back there."

Train No. 6, the *Exposition Flyer*, with No. 1803 on the point drifts downgrade near milepost 48 east of Tolland, Colorado.
— HENRY R. GRIFFITHS, JR.

16

Operation Saw-By

MOST OF the events you have read about so far involve other people and did not include me, personally. I will tell you of some "happenings" of my own. Like the first passenger train wreck I ever had a part in.

I was firing an M-78-class Mountain type jack for "Cautious Harry" Chambers on old No. 5 one night when we came up to a flag east of Sagers Siding. We hit two guns (track torpedoes) and slowed down as we approached a flagman who was waving a burning red fusee. We picked him up and eased on up to the red ABS (Automatic Block Signal) and stopped again. The crew of a 120-car long freight train had pulled into the 98-car passing track. Their head end was pulled out on the main line at the west switch to foul so that the caboose was in the clear of the main at the east end. A "saw-by." We were to pull our 12-car passenger train consist up between the switches on the main, then the freight crew would line the east gate and back their outfit up far enough to clear the west end and let us pass. A safe operation usually. Only on this occasion the student fireman on the freight drag misread a lamp signal and told his hoghead to back up before our

211

During June 1947, No. 3702 west rolls through Price River Canyon, Utah. This giant 4-6-6-4 is climbing Soldier Summit assisted by Nos. 3402 and 3509. — R. H. KINDIG

Extra No. 3705 east, another giant 4-6-6-4, tops the grade at Soldier Summit while the rear end helper, the No. 3601, keeps on shoving. — R. H. KINDIG

train was in the clear of the east switch. "Ker-Blam." The freight caboose collided with the sixth coach of No. 5 and turned that car over on the shoulder of the grade! It was just good fortune that no passengers were injured. The main line was tied up for several hours. Another call for the Big Hook.

After transferring our passengers from the rear coaches to the head end we proceeded on our westward way. At Maxwell Siding, just east of Helper, we had a red block thrown in our face. "Cautious Harry" was able to stop short of the signal and he got off the engine near the telephone booth. He instructed me to be ready to back up in the clear of the siding switch if anything showed up in Blue Cut. He said he would line the west switch for the pass so we wouldn't get hit on the nose. Sure as hell, no sooner had he placed the headset on his old grey head, than here came the headlight of an eastbound diesel freight train through the cut! I whistled back, got a signal and horsed her over. Harry ran for the switch and here came the second class train whose crew had not checked the train register against the arrival of a superior, first class train as required by the rules. What an eventful journey! A sideswipe and a headlight meet on the same trip! The "Brass" held two formal investigations on the same day, and discharged both of the freight train crews who were responsible for the various rules violations in connection therewith.

Here are some more "saw-by" experiences. One time I was mixed up in a "saw-by" operation that really took the prize for the number of trains involved, the length of time consumed, and the delays!

It happened during the early part of World War II when business was really heavy on the Rio Grande. We had about 30 freight pool crews assigned on the desert division. At this time we had three regular passenger trains in each direction and three regular freight, or second class daily schedules each way. Many trains were run as extras or as sections of a regular schedule. Some of the main or troop trains were run extra on a "Form G-Example Three" order and given right over all trains. With single track, ABS and timetable operation the subdivision was a madhouse. How the poor train dispatchers ever kept their sanity, I'll never know. It was not unusual to receive 50-60 copies of train orders on a single trip. There were 34 side tracks and 14 open

213

offices of communication on that 177 mile section of the railroad. Talk about busy! Each hoghead carried a clipboard for orders hanging on the boilerhead. You went over the road with your watch in one hand and the clipboard of "flimseys" in the other. We got along real well, too, in spite of the fact that there were many young runners, student firemen, and brakemen.

All of this is just a little background for the monumental foul-up at Vista Siding. Only a mile east of Thompson Springs, Vista was an abortion of a siding. It was just 63 car lengths long; it wouldn't hold any of the trains we were pulling in those days.

"Eddy" Christenson and I came east one afternoon on a drag of east line empties with a big Mallet for power. Those 3700-class

No. 3700 glides down the 2.4 percent grade through Castle Gate, on June 28, 1939. This famous landmark lost the left-hand portion of the Gate to a highway line change. — R. H. KINDIG

214

engines had 20,000 gallon water tanks. Remember this, 'cause it is important. We stopped in Green River for coal and water and to dope the rods. It is 27 miles to the top of the grade at Thompson and we used an hour and 50 minutes of hard work to get there, and were getting low on water. The old water spout at that station was located at the west end of the side track, near the telegraph office. After I filled the cistern we had to head in the siding for a superior, westbound hotshot. The operator had the board out, train orders for delivery to our train, only he was so busy with other matters he had not gotten a "complete" for us. So, we pulled on in the pass (passing siding), leaving our head man at the office (caboose) to bring the "flimseys" to our head end as soon as the overworked lightning slinger got them ready. The hotshot freight came and went.

It took a long time for old Jerry to walk 90-car lengths to reach our engine. He brought bad news. Our new instructions informed us that two Red Ball Extras West had right over our train from Grand Junction to Green River and that they would wait at Whitehouse, Elba, Sagers, and Vista until a specified time. Lordy, it took so long to get cleared and for the old man to deliver our running orders we had no time to make Sagers. We could go to Vista and clear the waiting time, but we could not clear the siding. Ninety cars in a 63-car length track leaves 27 hanging out on the main line. We went to Vista. We sawed the two RBX West, separately. Passenger train No. 8 came and went. Then No. 6 and No. 2. By then, because we had delayed these trains at Vista, No's 1, 5, and 7 were all late arriving at our location and were sawed in turn. This delayed several freight trains as well. In and out, in and out went our train. We stayed at Vista for eight hours! We let twelve trains go by. I was damn near out of water from all that switching. We made Grand Junction on the law, and never heard a word about the affair, never even got a letter. The "Brass" held a formal investigation for the Train Dispatcher and he was dismissed. It was really so simple to avoid the jackpot he got himself into. All he had to do was to set up a flat meet for us at Sagers and we would have gone there for the first two trains and been in the clear on a siding that would hold 90 cars.

Near dusk, Missouri Pacific's *Colorado Eagle* rolls south from Denver to Colorado Springs and Pueblo over the rails of the Denver & Rio Grande Western. In this scene at Pikeview, north of Colorado Springs, locomotive No. 7002 swiftly handles train No. 4. — DONALD DUKE

17

Highway Crossing Highlights

THE OLD Missouri Pacific *Colorado Eagle,* train Nos. 3 and 4 were a couple of red hot varnish jobs running between St. Louis and Denver. Sleek, new streamlined coaches and Pullmans pulled by three big E-8 diesel locomotives on the point. Those babies flew low and everything cleared for their passing.

One autumn day, at dusk, I boarded the engine on No. 3 at Colorado Springs to ride her into Pueblo with engineer Bert McElroy. We were ten minutes late out of the station because the Cheyenne Mountain Park Zoo had two crates of African lions for shipment to the zoo in St. Louis. Getting those big cats loaded took additional time, and that ten minute delay probably saved our lives. At least it prevented a bad accident.

Bert put me in the hot seat and we were rolling 70 miles per hour as we moved north of Widefield. All of a sudden a red flare bloomed in the growing darkness ahead. Since we were running on green signals and had busted no track signal torpedoes, I at once recognized that someone other than a railroad man was trying to warn our train. I went right after the electric brake, but at 70 m.p.h. a mile of distance disappears in just 50 seconds.

Here is railroad cooperation in motion. Missouri Pacific train No. 3, the *Colorado Eagle*, is handled by a Rio Grande crew on a joint Santa Fe-Rio Grande line between Pueblo and Denver. In this scene, the *Eagle* is just pulling into the AT&SF station in Colorado Springs. — DONALD DUKE

Shining silver and royal blue decorate the all new stainless steel cars of the Missouri Pacific's *Colorado Eagle* which ran over the rails of the Rio Grande in Colorado. This beautiful train operated on a fast overnight schedule between St. Louis and Denver in competition with the Union Pacific. — DONALD DUKE COLLECTION

As the E-8's headlight swung through a slight curve it illuminated a great, long stock trailer attached to a big GMC tractor right across the southward track. A frenzied trucker was waving a burning red fusee in a vertical raised and lowered position. This signal to a railroad man means "highball," or a come ahead signal.

I pulled the automatic brake valve handle from service to the emergency position and got out of the engineers seat. I stood on the deck bracing my shoulder against the controller and held on tight, ducking my head below the level of the front window, prepared to ride out the impending crash. At 35 miles per hour all of these speeding tons of passenger equipment plowed into the standing vehicle, spinning the tractor to the right and turning it over, parallel with our train but clear of the tracks. The trailer, loaded with calves, upset and broke open and the frightened cattle came boiling out, unhurt!

The train slid to a stop with fire flying from all the wheels. I got off the locomotive and went back to see just what we had hit, then to inspect our engine and see if all the passenger cars were still on the track.

It was a nerve shattering experience, and on inspection I found a small fire burning on the roadway crossing planks under our standing train. I climbed back on the rear diesel unit and got a fire extinguisher to douse the flames. Just as I finished that chore, the conductor, "Kid" Galloway, came up all out of breath and shaken. He was most excited. It seems that when the train stopped, the "Kid" got off the train to ascertain the reason for this unscheduled quick stop and was nearly run over by one of the frightened calves that had escaped from the wrecked trailer. When the conductor felt that hairy hide in the dark, he cried aloud,

"The lions are loose!"

There were no injuries. Except for some flat spots on the locomotive driving wheels there was no damage to the train, or track, but the truck was heavily damaged. Its driver had pulled off the main highway into the farm access lane to unload his stock. The rear dual wheels had dropped in the deep borrow ditch and he stalled, unable to go forward nor back. The tractor had stopped smack in the middle of the railroad track. So due to our delay at Colorado Springs loading the lions, it had given him the

Brand new Alco E-8 series 6000-class diesel locomotives powered the Missouri Pacific's *Colorado Eagle* between St. Louis and Denver in the late 1940's and into the early 1950's. — DONALD DUKE

extra time needed to get a flag out far enough to slow our speed by half. Otherwise we might have collided at 70 m.p.h. with more disastrous results.

The most feared and dreadful threat to any hoghead, or head end crew for that matter, is the gasoline delivery truck. A collision with one of those dragons is nearly always fatal. Many a railroad man has died in the fiery crash that ensues when the transport driver fails to stop, or tries to beat the onrushing train to the road crossing.

I've always thought that, in the event of an accident, my chances for survival were greater if I stayed in the cab and held on rather than to unload. Based on case histories, that seemed to be the safest course of action. I had previously practiced doing just that when threatened, except for the time when the double-bottom gas delivery behemoth stopped on the Gilsonite Crossing in the face of the speeding SPF, *California Fast Freight*.

When the Gilsonite processing plant was built at Loma the only highway access to the refinery was across the main line of the Rio Grande. The road entered Highway 50 at right angles and a stop sign required all of the outbound transports to come to a halt there, leaving part of their rigs foul of the railroad track.

I was firing for engineer Al Baxter, Jr. one bright spring morning and was doing the honors as hoghead when we roared down off Cavious Hill and shot 'round the curve in time to see a great blue monster, with two tanks trailing, pull out over the crossing and stop for the sign. He was one-mile away, and at our rate of speed, just 60 seconds from disaster. I jammed the automatic brake valve handle toward the right cab window, got out of the seat, opened the right side cab door, climbed to the bottom step of the side ladder, and all the while keeping my eyes on that obstruction to life and health. I vowed that if he did not clear the damn railroad track by the time we reached the ABS mast, which stood about one-quarter of a mile west of Purgatory, I'm gonna' drop off and take my chances with the birds!

As the rushing train slowed in full emergency, the truck driver moved his dangerous cargo clear of the crossing and I climbed back in the cab. Breathless, I might add. Afraid? You bet I was! Terrified, but still conscious of what to do in an emergency. I realized you just don't have long to recognize a condition and react. You must precondition your mind to get an immediate response.

Another time, while working as a fireman on the *California Zephyr*, we hit a stalled pickup truck down in Ruby Canyon. I had a good, daylight view ahead for about a mile when I spotted a vehicle on the track at a point where there was no established crossing. I yelled to my hoghead,

"Stop, there's a car on the track!"

He failed to grasp at once the fact there was a car where none should be and hesitated until he saw what I had been trying to tell him. When he finally recognized the object ahead he "plugged 'em," but too late to stop. The old clunker literally exploded under the 50 m.p.h. impact, with the cab of the pickup going off in one direction and the body in another. The hood flew up in the air and the motor literally jumped out of the frame. The four wheels departed in all directions and the glass showered our locomotive like a hail storm.

Thank God nothing went underneath to derail us. The owner of the wrecked vehicle was standing out by the right-of-way fence, waving his hat. He was too full of beer to give a damn.

Electro-Motive F-9, No. 5771, handles train No. 17, the *Rio Grande Zephyr*, through the tunnel district west of Plain, Colorado, in 1983. — RON C. HILL

18

Birthday Thrills and Chills

I HAVE FIRED and run an engine many miles in my lifetime and never had a serious passenger injury or fatality. In fact, on our railroad, the only passenger casualty to occur in a long time happened around 1943, during World War II. A serviceman, riding in a coach, was struck and killed by a falling rock in Gore Canyon. The rock came from high up on the canyon wall and hit the window of the car in which the man was riding. The train was only moving along at 25 m.p.h. at the time! Talk about blind luck, coincidence, or your freak accidents.

The *California Zephyr*, trains Nos. 17 and 18, were inaugurated in 1949 and had an excellent record for handling passengers in a safe and reliable manner. There have been incidents though. In one case, an engineer running No. 17 through Ruby Canyon ran into a section of washed out track which was caused by heavy rain on the desert. Evidently exceeding cautionary speed requirements, he derailed the entire train of four diesel units and 13 cars. There were no injuries, but quite a long delay.

The mountain side, near milepost 40, got real soft after a late thaw followed by a wet spring, and seepage of water appeared under the track. When No. 18 came sailing by one evening, the mud squished and squashed out from under the track and all four

223

When Amtrak was formed and the Burlington and Western Pacific gave up their passenger service, the Rio Grande continued to run the *California Zephyr* between Denver and Salt Lake City as the *Rio Grande Zephyr*. Train No. 17, with the No. 3109 and a steam generator car, stops at Granby, Colorado, station in 1978. — RON C. HILL

units of the locomotive turned over in Clear Creek, along with two trailing baggage cars. No one was hurt! The engine crew was tossed about in the cab of the rolling diesel locomotive, but both men were able to work the next trip. The engineer said,

"If you get bucked off, get right back on your horse if you ever want to be able to ride again."

A railroad enthusiast who was riding along in that cab on an authorized rail pass was so frightened by this experience that he vowed to take up a new hobby, and never again rode on a locomotive. Evidently he did not believe that "horse story."

It took two Big Hooks a couple of days of hard work to lift the EMD F-7 units back on their running gear, but not until a pair of bulldozers had push-pulled them out of the stream and close to the right-of-way.

In early March, another case involving No. 18 happened in Glenwood Canyon. Spring thaws and freezes alternate to pop rocks out of the overhanging cliffs and in this case caused a slide to occur. Engineer Bill Farmer hit just such a pile of boulders near

Shoshone, turning his four-unit consist upside-down and over the bank of the Colorado River. Luckily no one was injured. It was just a long, cold and frustrating experience. We had to use four GP-30's pulling on heavy cables assisted by a side boom dozer and two Big Hooks to lift the wrecked units up the 60 percent grade of the riverbank. One tough unit took 23 hours to raise it up to grade level before we could set it on its trucks. I don't know how many steel cables we broke in that operation, but I know that several failed.

One freezing night, the deep snow in Fraser Canyon put No. 18 (again!) in the ditch. Four units, four coaches, four feet of snow and four degrees below zero! The cars and units were all upright, just off the rails and slightly atilt. It took all night and until noon the next day to pick 'em up and restore train service. There were no injuries due to this accident, but one woman passenger, who was riding the train had a broken leg from a ski mishap and had to be carried a hundred yards to a relief train. I got to carry the heavy part, where the cast was. The Trainmaster took the lighter head end. Rank had its privileges.

Having had a long and eventful career it is difficult to select the event that gave me my biggest thrill, or which was the most frightening.

I guess I would have to say that the most thrilling, as well as memorable, experience of all came that snowy Christmas morning when the callboy rapped on my door and said,

"Dougherty, you are called for the No. 1509 to help No. 5 at 3:15 A.M. Your dad is the engineer." I had made a lot of student runs with the old "stack-rattler" as he was called, but this would be my first trip as his fireman. I was elated. I knew he could really get the work out of a big Mountain-type jack like the No. 1509 and I was anxious to show him that I could keep her hot and full of water for the battle with the grade on Soldier Summit.

I was born on December 25, 1917, just 21 years earlier. On that occasion dad had gone to the roundhouse and passed around a box of cigars, telling all the guys that if they needed a fireman old Santa Claus had just delivered one to his house. What a prophetic boast come true!

We hurried through breakfast and hastened to the coal chute where we got the old girl ready. Dad took his oil can with its long spout and a flaming kerosene torch, and got down on the ground to oil around and inspect her moving parts. I built up the fire and hosed down the deck and boiler head with the squirt hose. I checked everything twice. The water column was blown out and I tried the gage cocks and the water glass level. Then I looked at the "roof" (crown sheet) and checked for leaks or burned spots. Next I set the feeds on the hydrostatic lubricator. I tried both injectors and looked in the tank to make certain it was full of water. I also checked to see if we had a shaker bar, a wrench, a coal pick, hammer, grease gun, a flagging kit full of fusees, torpedoes and a red flag. The red and the white lanterns were filled and I fired their oil fed wicks with a kitchen match. Then I put the burning red one on the back of the tender for a tail light. Returning to the cab, I grabbed a handful of cotton waste and cleaned the steam and air gages. I wiped off the wind wings, the side windows, and dried the water off the seat boxes and arm rests. In those days, a fireman on a steam engine had a lot to do and twelve places to look if he wanted to earn the reputation of being a "good fireboy."

No. 5 roared into town on the advertised and the desert hoghead made a water spout stop. The hostler coupled our engine on the nose of the big 1800-class road engine, and dad got down to get the train orders the conductor brought him. After comparing time with the "Big O," he got back on his seat to wait for the carmen to signal for a brake test.

I must have been quivering with excitement when he finally whistled off and released the air brakes. Dad eased out on the steam throttle and let the reverse gear (Johnson Bar) down in full forward to start those mighty drivers turning. Chow. . .Chow. . . Chow, the thunderous exhaust quickened as he hooked her up on the quadrant and noise filled the world. I had a glass of water showing and the steam gage hand was on the "peg." Injector on and cut down fine. Duplex stokers auguring coal off the plates behind a 40-pound steam jet to feed the fire. I was ready.

There is no sound created quite like that, when two big jacks blast their challenge to the grade on a snowy morning! The thrill I felt was very much akin to a sexual experience. It did not really reach that same level of intensity, but it was embarrassingly close.

I kept the old girl stinking hot for the 25-mile run to the top of the hill. We made the running time of 50 minutes and he sure beat the stack off No. 1509 on that trip. I could tell he was proud of me and happy that I was going to follow in his footsteps. I enjoyed an exemplary career and had many promotions, but I was never the steam man my father was.

As I said before, I think that was my greatest railroad thrill. I got a big kick out of being promoted to engineer and very elated by my first trip as a passenger train hoghead, but those were anticlimactic by comparison.

I've been scared many times in my 41 years of railroading, by gasoline tankers and autos racing us to the crossings. Some of them also lost the race, and that too is frightening. Falling off and being run over at Pando was a scary experience. Meeting trains on the main track when one of you should be in the hole (siding). It's hairy, too, having hooks and cables break under the strain of lifting heavy cars and having broken ends and pieces flying about. Dropping cars without brakes and having derricks runaway on the hill is pretty horrifying. Once we were almost hit by an out of control engine. I've been around dynamite and rocket propellant as well as Army stuff, but my worst, and most frightening scare, was the wreck at Dotsero just before Christmas 1972.

Engineer Bill Clark on No. 71, hotshot westbound freight, had a spring hanger come down just as his speeding locomotive passed the west switch at Dotsero. The dragging hanger caught the stock rail and turned it over, derailing his three trailing units and nine cars. There were four trailer flats carrying eight highway trailers, all loaded with dressed beef quarters. They were followed by five big, white tanks of LPG (liquid petroleum gas) FLAMMABLE AND EXPLOSIVE! We were lucky that none of them ruptured; however, they did sustain pretty heavy damage and we had to be super careful not to puncture them as they were lifted back on their trucks.

A foot of snow covered the cedars and sagebrush and it was bone chilling cold. Everyone was anxious to finish with the job of rerailing the cripples so we could be home in time for the holidays. They really went all out to get the mess cleared. It was snowing hard as we put the hospital train together, getting ready for the long, slow ride back to Denver.

We had shoved the five cars of Propane into the east end of the

The *California Zephyr*, running between Chicago and San Francisco over the rails of the Burlington, Rio Grande, and Western Pacific, was often referred to as "The Most Beautiful Train in the Country!" The train, with four Vista-Dome cars each seating 24-passengers, was designed and scheduled for sightseeing. This is one of many brochures issued as a joint effort by the operating railroads during the years of the train. — DONALD DUKE COLLECTION

stock track to a joint with some of the other trailer flats. Suddenly one of the young trainmen rushed up to me all out of breath and shouted in his excitement,

"Mr. Dougherty, one of the Propane tanks has sprung a leak! I can hear the gas escaping!"

Jesus Christ, save us! This stuff is extremely volatile and I could visualize someone lighting a cigarette, or worse, the vapor rising high enough to be ignited by the hot coals in the firebox of the steam derrick. (This was before the Hooks were dieselized.) There were three train and engine crews on the scene, plus 25 or 30 carmen and section men as well as six or eight officers. All would be in a position of grave danger if the escaping gas ignited!

I was petrified with fright and yet knowing I had to do something. I shouted.

"Come on!" and went running along the string of cars looking for the leak. As we passed the derrick I could see the live coals on the grate.

I could hear the rush of escaping gas pressure. I could not breathe. For I was sure that any second now something would touch her off! My legs were as weak as water, but somehow I kept on going toward that terrible sound. Upon reaching the suspected car, I immediately relaxed. It was not gas escaping, which the lad heard, it was compressed air blowing from an open angle cock. Someone at the west end of the string of flats had coupled their engine on the cars and had opened the air line valve and let the brake pipe blow to atmosphere at our end. What a relief! Can you imagine what kind of a catastrophe would have resulted if five cars of high-bust gas had gone up in one terrific explosion?

We got the hospital train together and were all night long dragging it to Denver. We arrived around 08:00 Christmas morning. I never expected to see the dawn.

Retired Railroad Engineer Recalls Great Change In 46 Years of Service With Various Systems

HELPER—C. W. Dougherty, Helper, a veteran pioneer railroad engineer who has watched the progress of the railroads from, a cab in the engine for the past 46 years, has now retired and is spending his time visiting his many friends in Utah and Colorado.

An employe of the Denver & Rio Grande Western Railroad company since 1906, Mr. Dougherty has witnessed many changes on the railroad during his years of service.

Born in a log cabin in Philips county, Arkansas, on January 6, 1874, he started railroading at an early age. In 1888 he worked on the Little Rock & Memphis railroad, better known as the "Old Mud Line," at Hopefield, Ark. He was promoted to an engineer in 1897 while working on the St. Louis, Iron Mountain & Southern railroad at Little Rock and has spent very little time out of an engine cab since.

Knows Many Engines

He has worked on railroads running through 43 different states of the union during his 46 years of railroading. After working for the D & R G W railroad in 1906 Mr. Dougherty left for a few years and returned September 23, 1911, and worked for them until December, 1943, when he retired.

Mr. Dougherty has run many different types of engines—from the old Bogie on the Mexican Central to the latest Diesel engine type. Many changes have taken place. He remembers the shift from the old time tallow pot to the present force feed lubricator, and the cold water force pump

C. W. Dougherty . . . Has worked on railroads in 43 states.

to the present day exhaust steam injector.

Mr. Dougherty was the first man to run an engine on the Columbia branch of the railroad and on the Spring canyon branch when the railroad was building roads into the mining camps of Carbon county. He also helped build the Dotsero cutoff between Helper and Bond, Colo., and piloted the first engine through the Dotsero

cutoff upon completion of the project.

Proud of Children

Very proud of his children and stepchildren, Mr. Dougherty is inclined to boast of their accomplishments. Shortly after the arrival of his son, Sam, Mr. Dougherty was called for duty and upon reporting at the roundhouse told them if they needed a fireman for his engine the doctor had just left one at his home.

However, this came true, when 23 years later, Christmas morning, 1940, Mr. Dougherty was called to take an engine out to help a passenger train to Soldier Summit. The callboy told him that his fireman was S. A. Dougherty, Grand Junction, Colo.

Besides his son, he has a daughter, Almagene Dougherty, who is a stenographer in Salt Lake City, and three stepchildren, Fred Robinson and Althea Campbell, Salt Lake City, and Eleanor Moore, Carbondale, Colo.

On Mr. Dougherty's birthday, January 6, he was presented with a gift from the engineers with whom he had worked on the D & R G W railroad.

Possessing a lively sense of humor, Mr. Dougherty is very popular with his associates and can always be counted upon to relate the stories of his career. A pioneer in the railroading of Carbon county, he has set an enviable record for his son and others to follow. During 35 years' service with the Denver & Rio Grande Western he never received a reprimand and was considered one of their most valuable employes.

C. W. Dougherty, father of the author, was a "boomer" railroader. In railroad language a boomer is defined as a drifter who moved from one railroad job to another, staying but a short time on each job or each railroad line. Dougherty worked in 43 states during his 46 years of railroading (1888-1943), his last years were on the rails of the Denver & Rio Grande Western Railroad. The Salt Lake City _Telegram_, on February 23, 1944, honored this veteran for his contribution to the railroad industry.

— S. A. DOUGHERTY COLLECTION

19

Last Run

THERE WERE many highlights in my father's railroad career and great changes took place within his lifetime. He told me of the early days of using hardwood logs for fuel to fire his first steam locomotive. The engines had no headlights or air brakes then. A hand brake on the tender served to hold the little machine at rest after the hoghead stopped it with a vacuum type brake. The old man saw the motive power increase in size and tractive effort. Steam driven stokers replaced the scoop shovels, and air pumps and exhaust steam injectors were adopted for general use.

While working for the Rio Grande my dad ran locomotives on the work trains that built the Spring Canyon Branch, the Columbia Branch, and the Dotsero Cutoff. He was the first engineer to handle a passenger train on the new line running between Bond and Dotsero. The special train carried a private car occupied by the governor of the State of Utah who was to make a speech in celebration of the completion of the new rail link. The train was pulled by engine No. 782, a 4-6-2 type. A copy of the first train order ever issued for a train operating in that territory is reproduced herein.

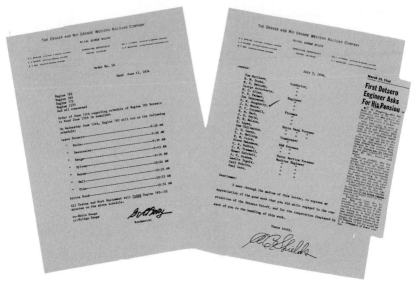

This is a copy of the first train order issued for a train movement on the newly completed Dotsero Cutoff, June 13, 1934. George E. Berry was Roadmaster in charge of construction. He had jurisdiction over train operation between Dotsero and Bond, Colorado. (RIGHT) The Rio Grande General Manager A. C. Shields wrote this letter addressed to all of the Rio Grande employees who had worked on the construction of the Dotsero Cutoff in 1934. The clipping is from *The Green Light*, the company's employee paper. — BOTH S. A. DOUGHERTY COLLECTION

Of my own experiences, aside from going to derailments, I served as an engineer on work trains engaged in construction of the Potash Spur in Eastern Utah. As an engineer, under a union contract, that was the last duty I performed for the railroad.

The next 16 years of my service was as a supervisor. I'm getting a little ahead of my story. I want to mention an incident that happened on what the Roadmaster called *Klondike Hill*. That is the name of a spur track on the branch between Brendel Siding and Potash Plant. Why it was called Klondike I will never know, since it is desert country. Temperature in the summer time runs around 120 degrees in the shade, and there are no trees within 25 miles of the location.

I had a GP-7 class EMD that was rated around 1,500 h.p. It was hotter than the hubs of hell outside as we shoved 16 loads of track material up the grade, making about 10 miles per, when all of a sudden the track ran off the road bed. A sun kink had moved the track to the left. The conductor and the Roadmaster, who were riding in the lead car of the cut, both pitched over the low side of the gondola and landed in the sand along the right-of-way. They were not injured, only surprised at the sudden turn of events. The gandy dancers repaired the damaged railroad and we backed up to take another run for the hill. We stalled before we reached the top. A second attempt and then a third produced the same results. On the fourth try, the Roadmaster established another Rio Grande "first." He fastened a long, steel cable to the rear end of a GMC truck (called a Jimmie diesel) and instructed the truck driver to start driving along the parallel roadway at a slow rate. We came charging up the grade, shoving our tonnage and as we lost our momentum, one of the gandys fastened the cable to a grab iron on the lead gon, and the truck double-headed us up the hill. That is the only instance I know where a highway vehicle performed "helping" service on our railroad.

I was involved with making two movies during my tenure as Road Foreman at Denver. I ran the locomotive in all of the action sequence in a thriller called *Runaway* starring Ben Johnson and Vera Miles. It was a lot of fun, even though the director of the film played a little trick on me.

The movie company used a helicopter to film long range action shots of the train as it "ran away" down grade in the tunnel district between Pine Cliff and Plainview Sidings.

The "chopper" pilot was a real pro. He could make that aircraft do tricks, and one of his stunts scared the hell out of me.

I was making like Ben Johnson, as he was cast in the role of the hoghead of the runaway ski special. The chopper was following our progress and the camera man was recording all of the action as the passenger train came flying down the two percent grade. The pilot would lift his machine just high enough to clear the top of the tunnels as the train bored through them.

As we came rushing out of Tunnel No. 3, there sat the helicopter sitting motionless in the middle of the track! I immediately grabbed for the automatic brake valve handle, figuring to "wipe the clock," when the movie director, who was standing beside my seat in the cab, put his hand on my hand and shouted in my ear, "No! No! It is allright, just a leettle joke!"

As the speeding locomotive drew near, the flying machine rose vertically with great quickness to just clear the top of our engine by a scant few feet. I was looking up as we passed beneath the chopper, and I could see the pilot's eyes, we were that close. Some joke. They scared me spitless. I had not realized a helicopter was so quick or so versatile.

I had a speaking part in a television special called *Make A Wish*. It ran about 15 minutes long and was filmed in and from the operating cab of the No. 5771 as the *Rio Grande Zephyr* departed Union Station in Denver, Colorado. I was wired for sound and the camera man shot the action, recording my comments as the train proceeded westward through some of the most spectacular mountain scenery in the world. The short feature was televised nationwide and was well received.

During my last three years of service on the railroad, I worked as Superintendent of Safety, Rules and Training. Part of my duties included investigation of personal injuries and accidents. I thought I had heard all of the alibies and excuses there were, but I was wrong. The new breed of employees were truly imaginative and original. A number of freakish things happened, but one event stands out above the rest.

A section laborer suffered a broken femur, but it was hardly an accident. You might say he broke it himself. Here is how it happened. Horseplay. He was making an explosive device, a bomb, which was comprised of two track bolts, a track nut and a couple of torpedoes. The man intended to set if off by dropping it from a bridge or another height. He started to screw one bolt in one side of the nut, put the powder from the torpedoes in the cavity of the nut and then started to screw the other bolt in on top of the charge. While holding the bolts in his hands to tighten them on the threads of the nut, he must have screwed too tight, because the thing blew up in his hands and the force of the explosion rammed the bolt head against his thigh hard enought to break the bone.

The three year period of my service in the Safety Department was interesting and rewarding, with the Rio Grande being awarded the Harriman Gold Medal for safety. The railroad won first place in the competition amongst the other railroads in our class. It was also my privilege and pleasure to help rewrite the Operating Rule Book and the Air Brake Manual. I also assisted with the new type of written tests for operating personnel. I held many classes for new employees, conducted examinations and issued promotions. In those classes, I recounted many of the personal experiences that appear in these pages as illustrations and examples of how to work safely. And of how to avoid the situations people create through inattention, ignorance of the rules or just plain knotheadedness. I hope that my efforts have kept some of the employees from getting killed or injured; that I have taught them how to do a good job of keeping the trains on time. And how to prevent those early morning calls for the Big Hook.

THE DYING HOG-HEAD'S LAST REQUEST
Jason Kelly

A hog-head on his death bed lay,
His life was ebbing fast away;
His friends around him closely pressed,
To hear the hog-head's last request.

He said "before I bid adieu,
One last request I'll ask of you;
Before I soar beyond the stars,
Just hook me on to a hundred cars.

"Oh, let me on that engine there,
Just to see how rough I can handle air;
Oh, let me at some water tank,
Make a 'big hole' stop and give a yank."

"Then from the corner of my eye,
I'll watch the pieces as they fly;
Then I'll calmly sit me down,
And watch the dust clouds settle round."

"Oh, let me pull a draw-bar out,
Then take my can with its long spout
And getting down upon the ground,
Take my own sweet time to oil around."

"Then far behind in that red caboose,
I'll hear the conductor turning loose
A few pet names as in days of yore
I've heard a thousand times before."

"Oh, just once more before I'm dead,
Let me stand the conductor on his head;
Let me see him crawl from beneath the wreck,
With a window sash hung around his neck."

"And when he comes and wants to fight,
Then I'll appear so innocent-like,
And the old excuse I will proclaim,
'There's a dynamiter in that train'"!!!

"And you, dear friends, I'll have to thank,
If you'll let me die at a water tank;
Within my ears that familiar sound,
The 'tallow-pot' pulling the tank spout down!"

"Oh, let me die holding in my hand
A bunch of waste and an old oil can;
Oh, let me die here on the ground,
Where I've spent the long years oiling around."

"Oh, let that train with the draw-bar down,
Have all of the crossings blocked in town;
And when they chain those cars together,
I hope it will be in sloppy weather."

"And when at last in my grave I'm laid,
Let it be in the cool of the water-tank shade;
And place within my lifeless hand
A 'monkey' wrench and an old oil can."

"A marble slab I do not crave,
Just mark the head of my lonely grave
With a draw-bar pointing toward the skies,
Showing the spot where this hog-head lies."

Then fainter grew the hog-head's breath;
His friends around him closely pressed.
His mind was wandering far away,
Perhaps to some other bye-gone day
When he was a hogger of great renown,
Was turning cabooses up-side-down.

Perhaps his mind was wandering back
To a draw-bar close beside the track
While he was trying to start the train,
And doing his best to break the chain.

Then his fact lit up in a joyful light,
And his sould prepared to take its flight.
His friends bent o're him and called his name;
He smiled and said, "I've broken the chain.'"
Then closing his eyes, he said no more;
He was doubling the hill to that other shore.

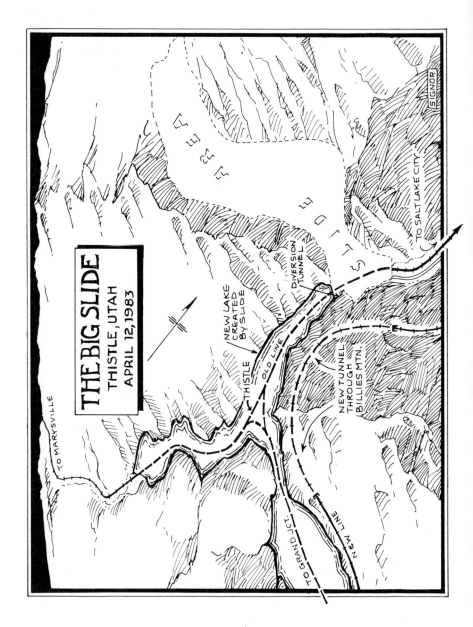

"RIO GRANDE RAILROAD BLOCKED BY SLIDE," read newspaper headlines in Utah and Colorado on April 14, 1983. It took a slide of gigantic proportions, as shown on this map, to stop the train movements on *The Action Road* here at Thistle, Utah.

20

The Big Slide

I N OVER 100 years of struggle against the forces of nature
and the failure of man, the Denver & Rio Grande Western
Railroad has never closed its lines for any extended period
of time, until April 14, 1983. On that date, just after train No. 18,
the *Rio Grande Zephyr* cleared Thistle, Utah at around 07:00,
both main tracks at that location began to heave, rise, and move
off the grade toward the Spanish Fork River. The entire slope of
the mountain, at the west end of the yard, commenced a slow,
inexorable movement downward into the stream. Caused by the
soaking of the earth from heavy winter snow and spring rains,
the mass of mud and rock continued sliding until it covered the
railroad right-of-way, Interstate Highway 6&50, and dammed the
river. Millions upon millions of tons of big rocks and dirt formed a
barrier that could not be moved or bypassed.

Through main line train movements came to a halt, stopped
cold. Highway traffic was rerouted through the Uintah Basin,
and the water trapped behind the natural dam inundated the
little village of Thistle to a depth of 160 feet! Rail traffic was
detoured over the Union Pacific, while all of the forces of the
railroad were directed toward building a new line on the north

side of the canyon above the level of the lake.

In a great burst of activity, a 3,100 foot long tunnel was bored through Billies Mountain. On July 4th, 81 days after this unprecedented act of nature, the first eastward freight train "highballed" through the slide blocked canyon, several hundred feet up the slope above the drowned junction point once called Thistle.

The Denver & Rio Grande Western Railroad was back in business!

The tragic fate of the little town of Thistle, Utah, became known throughout the country as newspapers, radio and television reports were distributed. The *Sun-Advocate* of Price, Utah, presented a very graphic presentation of the devistation in their April 22, 1983 edition.

Looking west from the new highway over Billies Mountain. At the left is the old rail line, the Spanish Fork River and the old highway. The new railroad is in the center and the new highway above on the right. All changes were made because of an act of nature, a monsterous mud slide which formed a dam across the river. — s. a. dougherty

View looking toward the east at Thistle. In the top left of this view is the deep cut through Billies Mountain for the new highway US 6 and 50. Twin railroad tunnels in the center are used to carry the rails of the D&RGW under the mountain. On the right is the slide blocking the river. — s. a. dougherty

Glossary of Words and Terms

A

ABS . . . An automatic block signal light on a mast.

ABS . . . An automatic block system: A series of consecutive block signals.

Air Brake . . . A mechanical brake used on cars, trains, and locomotives. It is actuated by compressed air pressure supplied through the brake pipe to operate rods, pistons, and levers to apply or release the train brakes.

Alley . . . A yard track. Clear alley . . . unoccupied yard track.

Alco . . . American Locomotive Company.

Alligator wrench . . . A heavy tool used to change air hoses on cars. The wrench has one smooth jaw and one serrated jaw.

Armstrong Method . . . Any hand operated task requiring muscle and sweat.

Ashcat . . . The fireman on a steam engine.

B

Banjo . . . A scoop shovel used by firemen on steam engines.

Bad Order . . . A defective car or locomotive. (Also a slang term for bowel movement, i.e. "set out a bad order.")

Ball the jack . . . Run fast . . . Scorch the ballast. Highball!

Barn . . . The enginehouse or roundhouse.

Beanery . . . Cafe for railroad men.

Beanery Queen . . . A waitress in the cafe or hash house.

Beans . . . Meal period. The proper hand signal given to indicate this is made by holding both hands extended with thumbs up, then alternately jabbing the thumbs toward the open mouth in rapid succession.

Big hole . . . Put the train brakes in emergency stop position.

Big Hook . . . The wrecker or more properly, the derrick used to pick up and rerail derailed cars and locomotives.

Big "E" . . . The locomotive engineer.

Big "O" . . . The train conductor.

Bird gang! . . . Unload . . . get off quickly as in an emergency.

Binder . . . Manually operated hand brake on a car.

Blind gaskets . . . A Stack of pancakes in the beanery.

242

Blow-off cock . . . A manually operated valve located in the cab of a steam engine used to vent boiler sludge into the atmosphere.

'Bo . . . Hobo or tramp. A free rider.

Boney . . . An inferior grade of coal, usually refuse from a mine.

Boomer . . . An itinerant railroad worker . . . a well traveled man.

Brains, The . . . The train conductor.

Brain Box . . . The caboose of the train where the Brain rides.

Brake club . . . A three foot length of ash wood used to set hand brakes on cars left standing on grades. The club provided additional leverage to put more pressure on the brake shoes.

Brass . . . Railroad officials . . . also called brass hats.

Brownies . . . Demerits conferred on an employee's personnel record under the *Brown System* of discipline used by many railroads.

Bug dust . . . Poor quality fuel and very dusty . . . low B.t.u. content.

C

Cage . . . The train caboose. Sometimes called the squirrel cage.

Callboy . . . Sometimes just "caller." The employee assigned to keep the crew lists (boards) and call the crews for service in their proper turn. First-in-First out.

Can . . . A tank car.

Canned . . . Dismissed from service . . . sacked . . . "tied a can on."

Car toad . . . Car inspectors, or mechanics.

Carry the green . . . Display signals for a following section of that schedule. Two green flags by day and two green lights by night on the front of the locomotive.

Cat . . . A versatile machine made by Caterpillar Tractor Company.

Cinder chewers . . . Conductors, trainmen, switchmen. Those who work on the ground in the cinders, throwing switches.

Civil engineer . . . A hoghead who had been dismissed.

Cinder Dicks . . . Railroad Special Policemen.

Clinker hook . . . A long, heavy rod with a claw on the one end and a handle on the other. Used for cleaning fire boxes of steam locomotives.

Consist . . . The train manifest as to loads, empties and tons.

Cripple . . . A disabled or defective car or locomotive.

Crummy . . . The train caboose—also crum box.

CTC . . . Centralized traffic control system of train operation.

Cupola . . . The top section of a split-level construction of a caboose designed to give the rear end crew a better view of their moving train.

D

Deadhead . . . Sleep going and work coming back. Also a term applied to free riders or lazy employees.

Deadman . . . A buried anchor post for a chev or pulley used in pulling heavy equipment back to grade level.

Deadman pedal . . . A safety device on diesel locomotives that will automatically apply the train air brakes if the engineer takes his foot off the pedal.

Detainer . . . The train dispatcher.

Dog catch . . . A call to deadhead to relieve a crew whose working time has expired under the "Dog Law."

Dog hosue . . . The small wooden cubicle built on top of the water cistern of a steam engine. The dog house provides a shelter for the head brakeman to ride in and where he has a good view to inspect his train for hot boxes or dragging equipment.

Dog Law . . . The Adamson Law which limits the legal hours of service for operating crews to 16 continuous hours—now 12 hours because of a recent change in the law.

Double-header . . . Two locomotives coupled at the head end of a train.

Drink . . . Water for the steam boiler.

Drop . . . A switching move (short-cut) whereby a car is cut off in motion and allowed to drift into an adjacent track.

Dwarf block . . . ABS on a short mast . . . a ground level signal.

Dynamiter . . . A defective air brake control valve that acts to put the train brakes in emergency—"in the big hole."

Dynamiter . . . A dissenting vote at the union meeting, or as applied to a complaining, disgruntled employee. A trouble maker.

Dynamic brake . . . A traction brake on the diesel locomotive used to retard train speed on descending grades without the use of air brakes.

E

Eagle Eye . . . The sharp-eyed engineer.

Easy sign . . . Slow down . . . reduce speed. Prepare to stop.

EMD . . . Electro Motive Division of General Motors Corp.

Extra board . . . Spare man list where an employee with little seniority waits for the old head regular man to lay off and give him a trip. Sometimes called slow board.

F

Field man . . . A yard switchman who works the long field as opposed to the pin puller who works near the engine.

Fixed signal . . . A signal of a fixed location indicating a condition affecting the movement of a train or locomotive.

Fixed signal . . . An immobile student brakeman on top of a box car, in the dark, and with his lantern unlit.

Flag . . . The act required to provide flag protection for a train or engine under the provisions of Operating Rule 99.

Flag . . . The a/k/a or alias used by a boomer railroad man.

Flat . . . A car having a deck, but no ends, top or sides.

Flat wheel . . . One that has been skidded or slid to create flat spots.

Freezer . . . A refrigerator car. Also reefer or icer.

Frog . . . A big, heavy part of a track switch where cars are frequently derailed.

Frog . . . A big, heavy device used to rerail derailed equipment.

Fusee . . . A signal flare, either red or yellow, used to give warning signals.

G

Galloper . . . A high-wheeled, fast running locomotive.

Galloping fat . . . Engine oil . . . lubricant.

Gandy dancer . . . A track laborer, so called on account of the rhythmic motion of tamping ballast under the crossties with a shovel which made him look as though he was dancing. The tool was from the Gandy Manufacturing Company.

Garden . . . A train yard where the color switch lights look like flowers blooming in the dark.

Gate . . . A track switch.

GMC . . . General Motors Corporation, builders of diesel locomotives.

GM . . . General Manager of the railroad . . . the "high brass."

Goat . . . Yard switching engine . . . shunter. Also yard goat.

Gon . . . A steel sided car. Short for gondola-type car.

GP-30 . . . A general purpose diesel locomotive.

Grab iron . . . The hand holds attached to the ends and sides of
railroad cars to provide a place to ride on moving equipment
and give access to the top of the car.

Guns . . . Torpedoes . . . Flat pieces of dynamite that, when
strapped to the top of the rail, will explode with a loud bang
when run over by the wheels of a car or engine.

H

Hand bomber . . . A hand fired steam engine.

Hash house . . . See beanery.

Hay burner . . . A hand lantern that burned kerosene for light.
The lantern globe was always blackened, needed cleaning and
was difficult to see in the dark.

Head in . . . Take the siding, go in the hole, clear the main track.

Head man . . . the trainman who rode the front end of the train.

High Ball . . . Proceed—Go, go fast. Everything is OK.

High green . . . Clear signal on the main line.

High Iron . . . The main track . . . a romantic term.

Hogger . . . The locomotive engineer in charge of and responsible
for the operation of the locomotive as required by the rules.

Hoghead . . . Another pet name for an engineer.

Hog Jockey . . . Same guy.

Hog Law . . . Same as Dog Law . . . Federal Hours of Service
Law.

Hole . . . The siding, a track adjacent to the main track, used for
meeting or passing trains. Also a passing track.

Hook . . . As in the Big Hook . . . the derrick or wrecker.

Hook . . . As in making a hook or joint . . . a coupling to another
car.

Horse over . . . pull the Johnson Bar in reverse, an act guaranteed
to slide the drivers and create flat spots on them.

I

In the clear . . . On a siding, clear of the main track or clear of the fouling point of a yard track.

In the ditch . . . Equipment derailed. Off the track, sometimes turned over and damaged.

Ingersol . . . A non-standard watch carried in fob or bib of overalls.

Iron . . . As in rails, switch points. To bend the iron means to operate, or line a track switch.

J

Jack . . . a slang term for locomotive.

Jack-leg . . . Cheap or phoney imitation of the real article.

Jerry-built . . . A cheap, temporary repair or construction.

Johnson Bar . . . The reversing lever on steam engines. A means of regulating steam pressure to the pistons by reducing the lap and lead of the valves.

Join the birds . . . Get off quick! Leave now.

Juice Jack . . . A diesel electric locomotive.

Junk pile . . . an ancient steam engine in poor shape mechanically.

K

Kangaroo Court . . . A formal investigation.

Keeley can . . . A five gallon can tied to the side of a car over a hot journal box so cold water from the container could be fed to the overheated part to provide cooling for it en route.

Keeley line . . . A one-quarter inch copper line on a steam engine used to convey water from the cistern to the running gear. Flow of water was regulated by valves and used to cool overheated crank pins and driving boxes.

Keeley cure . . . Re-habilation for alcoholics. Go on the water wagon.

Kick . . . A switching move (shortcut) . . . see drop.

King Snipe . . . The section boss.

Knuckle . . . The moveable part of a car coupler, called a drawbar.

Knuckle buster . . . Either a defective alligator wrench or a careless hoghead, well known for breaking trains in two.

L

Ladder . . . The principal lead in a switching yard.

Lap order . . . When the train dispatcher gives two opposing trains right of track over each other. A sure-fire way to cause a head-on collision.

Light engine . . . A locomotive running without cars or caboose. A move used to equalize motive power distribution on a division.

Lightning slinger . . . Telegrapher or train order operator.

Loads . . . Freight cars under lading of various commodities.

Lung . . . A car coupler. Pulling a lung out meant a break in-two.

L/V . . . Lateral/Vertical forces of track-train dynamics.

M

Main train . . . A special passenger train carrying Naval or Military personnel. Any troop movement.

Markers . . . The tail lights on a caboose that indicate to other trains that the train is all there, a complete unit. "You never met a train until you met his markers."

Mike . . . A 2-8-2 type of steam locomotive called a Mikado. The first of their type were built for export to Japan.

MM . . . The master mechanic.

Mtys . . . Empty cars.

Mud hop . . . A yard office clerk or number grabber.

Muzzle loader . . . A hand fired steam engine.

N

No bill . . . An employee who was not affiliated with a railroad union. See scissor bill.

No bill . . . A freight car moving over the railroad without the proper way bill.

Nut splitter . . . A roundhouse mechanic.

Number dummy . . . A yard office clerk.

O

Oil can . . . A railroad tank car.

Old Man . . . The Division Superintendent or the General Manager.

Old Girl . . . An affectionate term for a steam engine. Sometimes called Girl . . . They were all called "she" because they wore skirts on the tank and had petticoat pipes in the smoke box (front end).

Old hand . . . Either of these terms meant an experienced man.

Old head . . . See above.

ORC . . . Order of Railroad Conductors. (Railway?)

Order board . . . A semaphore type signal used at train order offices to indicate to crews whether there were orders for delivery to their train.

Outlawed . . . A car or locomotive that had not received Federal Inspection within the required time frame. Or a crew that had exceeded the Federal Hours of Service Law.

P

Paper heads . . . Yard office personnel. Secretaries.

Petticoat pipe . . . An extension of the stack that comes down in the smoke box. Sometimes called a stack liner, it fits over the exhaust nozzle and creates a vacuum necessary for proper draft on the fire.

Pig . . . A derogatory term for steam engine.

Pig head . . . Ditto for the engineer.

Pike . . . A railroad line.

Pin dope . . . A type of hard grease used to dope (lubricate) the side rod connections and crank pins of a steam engine.

Pin heads . . . Derogatory term for trainmen.

Pops . . . In one usage they are pressure retaining valves. A feature of the air brake system whereby pressure is retained in the car brake cylinders to hold the brakes applied at the same time the brake pipe and auxiliary reservoir pressures are being restored.

Pop valve . . . A pressure relief valve on the locomotive boiler used to maintian no more than maximum working pressure.

Pull the air . . . To set the train air brakes by use of the manually operated valve located in the caboose of freight trains and in the end compartments of passenger coaches.

Pull the pin . . . Quit. Resign.

R

Rails . . . Railroad employees.

Real estate . . . Poor quality coal . . . boney.

Red block . . . Stop signal indication.

Red Board . . . Train orders for delivery. Either pick up on the fly or stop to obtain a clearance on the board.

Reefer . . . A refrigerator car. Also called icer.

Reptile . . . A yard switchman. See snake.

Right hand side . . . The engineer's seat box location.

Rip rap . . . Large rocks or concrete slabs used to protect the sub-grade of the track against flooding at exposed places.

Rock . . . On ones paycheck . . . a garnishment. Demand for payment.

Rule "G" . . . The use or possession of narcotics or alcohol by employees on duty is prohibited.

Rule 99 . . . The rule that requires flag protection for a train or locomotive under certain conditions.

Run around . . . When one train passes another en route . . . see "spiked."

Runaround . . . To mishandle the crew list (board) by calling the second out crew ahead of the first out crew, thereby depriving them of their proper turn.

Runaway . . . A car, train, or locomotive moving out of control.

S

Sandhouse talk . . . Rumor or scuttlebutt. Idle gossip.

Saw-by . . . Two trains meet or pass each other at a siding that is too short to accommodate the longest train.

S-B . . . A bulldozer equipped with a side-mounted boom that is used in wrecking operations.

Scissor bill . . . Same as no bill.

Scab . . . A strike breaker. Non-union employee.

Scoop . . . A type of shovel used by firemen on steam engines.

Sea shore . . . The sand applied to the rails to improve traction. As in "two pipes to the . . ."

Shack . . . a brakeman.

Shaker bar . . . A long, heavy rod used to shake the fire box grates on a steam locomotive.

Snake . . . A yard switchman . . . so named for the big, blue "S" on Switchman's Union of North America lapel button.

Squirt hose . . . A short length of rubber hose connected to the feed water pump or injector of a steam engine and used to wash off the deck and boiler head (and occasionally the engineer's feet, accidentally, of course).

Stump puller . . . A small, ineffective derrick.

Sun kink . . . Heat expansion of the rails causes the track to move, buckle and bend. Usually results in a derailment.

T

Tallow pot . . . Either an oil can or the poor old fireman.

Throne . . . The engineer's seat on the locomotive.

Torpedoes . . . Pieces of dynamite wrapped in red paper and provided with lead straps attached to hold the explosive charge on top of the rail. When compressed by the wheel of a car or locomotive the torpedo goes off with a loud bang to alert the engineer of a flagman ahead.

Track monkey . . . The roadmaster.

Train Line . . . Same as Brake pipe. See Air Brakes.

U-V

Unload . . . Get off quickly, as in an emergency.

Varnish . . . A passenger train.

W

Wash out . . . A frantic signal given to stop the movement.

Wipe the clock . . . Go to emergency position. "Big hole 'er."

Wye . . . A track layout built in the shape of a "Y" and used to reverse equipment, i.e. "turn on the wye."

Z

Zebras . . . Highway Patrolmen and City Policemen in black and white painted automobiles who come immediately when your train is blocking a street or road crossing, but take all day to respond when you strike an automobile.

Index

Biographical Index

Subject Index